American Interiors

NEW ENGLAND and the SOUTH

Donald C. Peirce

and

Hope Alswang

PERIOD ROOMS AT THE BROOKLYN MUSEUM

Exclusively distributed to the trade by UNIVERSE BOOKS, New York

Designed and published by The Brooklyn Museum, Division of Publications and Marketing Services, Eastern Parkway, Brooklyn, New York 11238. Printed in the USA by Conceptual Litho Inc., New York.

Exclusively distributed to the Trade by **Universe Books** 381 Park Avenue South New York, New York 10016

ISBN-0-87273-095-6
Library of Congress Catalog No. 82–74299
© 1983 The Brooklyn Museum
This publication is made possible in part by a grant from the National Endowment for the Arts, a Federal agency

INTRODUCTION

The Period Room: An Illusion of the Past

Dianne H. Pilgrim
Curator of Decorative Arts
The Brooklyn Museum, New York

On December 2, 1929, nineteen American period rooms were opened to the public at The Brooklyn Museum. From their inception they have been the central focus of the Department of Decorative Arts, and one of the most popular exhibits in the Museum. Today the Museum's installation includes twenty-eight rooms ranging in date from a 1675 Dutch house from Flatlands, Brooklyn, to a 1928 Art Deco library from a New York Park Avenue apartment. In many ways these rooms are unique and among the first of their kind.

The idea of the period room is relatively new. It originated in nineteenth-century Europe with a fundamental change in the philosophy of museum installations. The impetus for this change came from many different sources, such as national and ethnic pride, and took many diverse forms: panoramas, dioramas, wax exhibits, and natural history habitats. Museum displays gradually began to be organized by style or period rather than by material. Once this transition of thought had been made, the idea of period settings was a logical development.

Americans were slow to gain an appreciation of their own culture. Although there were individual examples of buildings saved and collectors of Americana before 1900, the mania for collecting our colonial past did not begin in earnest until the teens and twenties. The Essex Institute in Salem, Massachusetts, installed three period rooms in 1907, but the first American art museum to organize a large and systematic collection of period rooms was New York's Metropolitan Museum, which opened its American Wing in 1924. Of course, scattered examples of period rooms already existed in other institutions, but the American Wing had a profound effect on museums and collectors everywhere. Shortly thereafter museums in Philadelphia (1928), Boston (1928), Brooklyn (1929), Baltimore (1930), and St. Louis (1930-31) proudly displayed their own rooms.

Period rooms are paradoxical, posing problems for every institution that has inherited them from the past. Is the room a fantasy or is it a fairly accurate approximation of the past? Is the point of view historical or aesthetic? What is the room trying to show or prove? No matter how hard one tries, it is impossible to eliminate the influence of one's own time and taste upon one's concept of the past. A period room is inescapably an illusion.

The Brooklyn Museum's rooms have been renovated and reinterpreted a number of times since 1929 as new scholarship has evolved. Each time the installations have been considered more accurate approximations of the past. Still, as can be seen in this book's photographs of the various attempts, including the most recent, the rooms have always said as much about the moment of installation as they have about the periods they strive to depict.

Museums, on the whole, have been negligent in informing the public as to what it is seeing in period rooms. But until recently very little had been written on period rooms and few criteria for interpreting them had been established. Each institution had a different set of circumstances and, therefore, a different set of solutions.

The Brooklyn Museum has inherited rooms with three remarkable features that have influenced the philosophy and treatment of the rooms over the years. One of these features is the rooms' degree of architectural accuracy. Few changes were made in the dimensions of the rooms when they were installed in the Museum. Since period rooms were originally collected not so much for their architectural and historical importance as for their attractiveness as backdrops for furniture, this concern for accuracy is quite unusual. The second unique feature of the rooms is their arrangement by region—an innovation that was praised by the press at the time of the opening in 1929. Reporters seemed intrigued that comparisons could be made between the architecture of New England, the South, and the Middle-Atlantic states. This concern for architecture also resulted in the period room series' third major distinction—the installation, in many cases, of entire ground floors. It was hoped that wherever possible the visitor would have the impression of being in a house, not in a room isolated from its original position.

The guiding spirit behind The Brooklyn Museum's period rooms and its collections of American decorative arts in general was Luke Vincent Lockwood (1872-1951), the noted author and early collector of Americana. Lockwood joined the Museum's Board of Governors in 1914, the year the Museum created a department of "Colonial and Early American Furniture." Although two mantels and a doorway were acquired that year, it was not until the following year that the first room—actually a pastiche—was purchased. Although a series of period rooms was envisioned from the beginning, their final installation was not possible until the Museum building was enlarged and completed in 1927. Over the next two years, under Lockwood's direction, Andre Rueff, the Assistant Curator from 1912 to 1933, supervised the rooms' installation.

Lockwood's philosophy, scholarship, and integrity set the standard for all future renovations and additions to the rooms. The first major refurbishing occurred in the 1940s under John Graham, who was Curator from 1938 to 1949. Furniture arrangements, upholstery, and floor and window treatments were changed according to current scholarship. Perhaps Graham's most significant contribution was his attempt to determine the rooms' original paint colors. With the exception of the Cupola House hall and parlor, the Cane Acres Plantation dining room, and the Bliss House chamber, all the rooms had been painted white when they were opened in 1929. Fortunately, most of the woodwork in the houses, except for that in the Trippe and Cupola House stairhalls, had never been stripped. Graham was able to accurately restore most of the rooms to their original colors. This was no mean feat considering how difficult the task is even today with the aid of modern technology.

Graham also had tremendous foresight in acquiring a number of rooms from nineteenth-century houses (dating to 1836, 1853, *circa* 1877, and 1882) for future installation. There was very little interest in nineteenth-century American decorative arts and architecture before the 1970s. In fact, Brooklyn was the first American art museum to install a series of nineteenth-century period rooms. This was done in 1953 under the direction of Curator Charles Nagel (then also Director of the Museum) and Victor Proetz, an interior designer.

The Museum installed its earliest rooms—the 1675 Jan Martense Schenck House—in 1964. Four years later, the man responsible for this installation, Curator Marvin D. Schwartz, wrote a book on the period rooms entitled *American Interiors*. Although this was not the first book on the rooms (a small brochure that had come out in 1930 was expanded by Assistant Curator Elizabeth Haynes in 1936), it was the most extensive, serving as an excellent guide to both the rooms and the collection.

In 1970 Curator J. Stewart Johnson acquired the 1928 Worgelt Library, perhaps the first twentieth-century period room in an American art museum. The room was installed in 1971. Johnson also installed new galleries devoted to nineteenth- and twentieth-century decorative arts.

The 1980 renovation of the New England and Southern rooms that this book documents was undertaken for numerous reasons. More than thirty years of New York City grit had accumulated, the 1929 sheet rock ceilings were sagging, the lighting and labels were inadequate, the public viewing cages were antiquated, and storage space was needed. The philosophy behind the renovation was to continue Lockwood's tradition of presenting as accurate an approximation of the past as possible despite the inherent limitations of such an approach. Throughout, an attempt was made to illustrate the range of choice—in fabrics, window and floor treatments, furniture, and accessories—that was available during the eighteenth century in a given location. Care was taken to reflect the original owners of each house, their standing in the community, and the house's location.

Despite these attempts at historical accuracy, the rooms are still only broad statements about a certain time and place, with an emphasis on style. In most of the rooms, only the woodwork is original. Most of the fabrics used in decorating and upholstery are reproductions, and Museum replacements have been used for the plaster walls, the fireplace interiors, and all of the floors except those in the Bliss and Cane Acres rooms. With the exception of the furniture in the Porter-Belden House, none of the furnishings in the current installations were in those rooms during the eighteenth century. Eighteenth-century rooms were rarely furnished in a single period style as the Museum's rooms tend to be.

When research for the 1980 renovation was begun in 1976, it became apparent how little is yet known about eighteenth-century American interiors. It is not easy to obtain answers from books to such complex problems as room arrangements, upholstery, floor and window treatments, and paint colors. Although estate inventories (which are available for a number of the Museum's rooms) are useful for ascertaining a person's possessions, they provide no help in determining how those objects were used and where they were placed. There are few written descriptions of interiors and little known pictorial evidence. Eighteenth-century American painting consisted primarily of portraits, which can be useful as far as providing information about the treatment of upholstery but are of little help otherwise. Since the original owners of the New England and Southern period rooms were English or of English descent, it seemed logical to rely on English pictorial documentation.

Few museum period rooms compare with Brooklyn's in quantity, architectural accuracy, time span, and geographical range. But the importance of period rooms varies from institution to institution, and there is certainly no single correct approach to their installation. For museums that inherited this early twentieth-century mode of displaying decorative arts, the challenges are enormous. Other methods have developed over the years for effectively showing decorative arts to their best advantage. Still, the period room remains an important tool for the graphic illustration of the history, mores, and art of Americans.

The Museum is indebted to many individuals and institutions for their assistance in making the 1980 renovation project and this book about it possible. We are extremely grateful to the National Endowment for the Arts and the Sack Foundation for their support of both, and to E. Martin Wunsch, Mrs. Hollis K. Thayer, and Henrietta Blau for their generosity in support of the renovation.

Over the past six years assistance and cooperation have been received from countless colleagues. I would like to thank everyone, and particularly the following: Father Robert H. Biad; Georgianna Contiguglia of The Denver Art Museum; Stephen Gemberling; Mary Graham; Margaret U. Ferris; Lou Hafermehl and Rosa E. Davenport of Historic Edenton, Incorporated, in Edenton, North Carolina; Daniel M. C. Hopping; Ruth Johnston-Feller; Henry Joyce; Mildred Lanier of Colonial Williamsburg in Williamsburg, Virginia; Florence Montgomery; Elizabeth V. Moore; Kevin Sweeney of The Webb-Deane-Stevens Museum in Wethersfield, Connecticut; Barbara Teller; Neville Thompson and the staff of The Henry Francis du Pont Winterthur Museum Library in Winterthur, Delaware; Gudmund Vigtel and Katharine Gross Farnham of The High Museum of Art in Atlanta, Georgia; and Edward F. Zimmer.

I am grateful to the students from Columbia University's Historic Preservation Program who wrote papers on the rooms in 1976 and '77. Their research was invaluable.

For their hard work and support throughout this project, I would like to thank the following members of the Museum's Department of Decorative Arts: Robert Ferguson, Carol Krute, Diane Quero, Kevin Stayton, Celestina Ucciferri, and Christopher Wilk. My thanks also to Ann Coleman, the Museum's Curator of Costumes and Textiles, and to Sue Sack and Dan Kushel of the Museum's Conservation Department.

Lastly, I would like to thank Donald C. Peirce, now Curator of Decorative Arts at The High Museum, and Hope Alswang, now Curator of The Society for the Preservation of Long Island Antiquities, who worked on the renovation of the period rooms and wrote this book. The reality and integrity of the rooms are due to their intelligence, imagination, and persistence.

Trippe House hall (left) during construction in 1976 (the area above the Southern period rooms was strengthened with steel beams so that it could be used for storage); and a 1975 file photograph (right) showing the antiquated public viewing cage and inadequate lighting system.

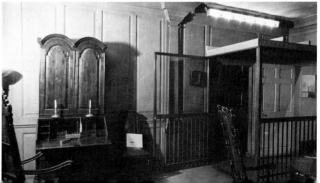

The Danbury Alcove, *here used to exhibit a century of chairmaking in America.*

Below: *These photographs of the Danbury Alcove woodwork laid out on* the Museum's basement floor in 1915 reveal that elements presently in the installation—such as the windows, the bolection molding around the fireplace opening, and some of the cornice—were not part of the original purchase.

The Danbury Alcove 18th Century

Danbury, Connecticut

The Danbury Alcove (or Dining Room, as it was originally called) constitutes the first woodwork acquired by The Brooklyn Museum. With its acquisition in 1915, the Museum became one of the first in the country to see the period room as an effective means of displaying American decorative arts.

Because there were only a few period rooms known at that time (the most publicized being the three alcoves set up in 1907 by the Essex Institute in Salem, Massachusetts), the Museum had no established criteria or philosophy to guide it in this initial acquisition. As a result, the Danbury Alcove differs in significant respects from the series of American interiors that evolved at the Museum over the next fourteen years. Unlike future acquisitions, in which woodwork was often purchased directly from the owners of buildings and removed under the supervision of Museum personnel who carefully coded the architectural elements for reconstruction, the alcove was acquired second-hand—from George Ives, a pioneer dealer of Americana in Danbury, Connecticut. Whereas in following acquisitions the Museum tried whenever possible to obtain the woodwork in its entirety, what was bought in this case was not really a room at all but woodwork consisting of a fireplace wall, two walls of wainscoting, and a corner cupboard or "boffet." Of all the interiors, it is the only one for which not even a general provenance is known, since Ives could not identify the house from which it came.

At its opening in 1929, the installation was called the Danbury Dining Room, perhaps because of Ives' place of business. The woodwork was white, and behind the windows were painted dioramas of blue skies and green hills, with branches and artificial leaves.

Early nineteenth-century New Jersey-type chairs were placed around a William and Mary table, and glass, ceramics, and pewter ranging in date from 1750 to 1850 completed the setting. The paint color and the efforts at quaintness had more to do with an early twentieth-century collector's taste than with the taste of an eighteenth-century Connecticut farmer.

In the 1940s, when John Graham scraped paint from the fireplace wall and discovered traces of dark red, the

1929 installation

woodwork was repainted that color. Graham also replaced the New Jersey-type chairs with eighteenth-century Connecticut examples and had curtains made from eighteenth-century European printed cotton. In the ensuing years, additional objects were placed in the space, and the installation was presented as a rural New England keeping room.

Recent examination of the woodwork has given rise to further questions regarding the alcove's proportions, since the size and height do not relate to any known existing eighteenth-century interiors. Also in question is the relationship between the various elements of the room and whether they were in fact together in the eighteenth century. Indeed, some elements, including the cornice and the windows, were obviously made at the time of the 1929 installation.

Because of its importance as the first woodwork acquired by the Museum, the paneling was retained in the 1980 renovation. Yet because the questions regarding the space had made it difficult to consider the alcove in the same manner as the rest of the Museum's period rooms, it was converted from a period room installation to an exhibition case. Graham's red paint was kept and cleaned and the floor was painted in black and white blocks—an eighteenth-century treatment that simulated cut and laid stone. Although it is impossible to know how frequent this practice was, fragments of paint applied in a similar manner survive in the parlor of the eighteenth-century Van Cortlandt Manor in Croton, New York. Early-American portraits like the one of Robert Gibbs reproduced here also indicate an interest in decorated floors, although in this painting the floor may be an example of painterly convention.

This renovation provides additional exhibition space for the Museum's collection and clearly distinguishes the space from the archaeologically correct rooms in the Museum.

1940s installation photographed in 1965

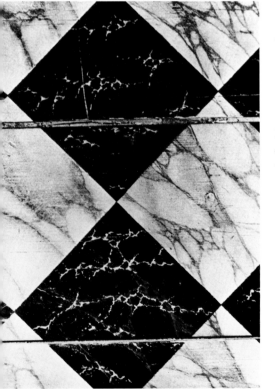

Left:
The parlor floor at Van Cortlandt Manor in Croton, New York

PHOTO: SLEEPY HOLLOW RESTORATIONS, TARRYTOWN, NEW YORK

Right:
Attributed to the Freake limner
Portrait of Robert Gibbs *1670*
Oil on canvas
Collection: Museum of Fine Arts, Boston (The M. and M. Karolik Collection)

Exterior of the Reuben Bliss House circa *1920*

NEW ENGLAND

The Reuben Bliss House
CIRCA 1750

Springfield, Massachusetts

Springfield was established on the banks of the Connecticut River in western Massachusetts in 1636 and incorporated as a town in 1641. A center of Indian hostilities during initial settlement of the area, it was an important outpost on the seventeenth-century frontier. The town again came to prominence during the American Revolution, when an arsenal established there in 1777 became a military supply depot for the Continental Army. Throughout the eighteenth century Springfield was a commercial center for its section of the Connecticut River Valley and the area's rapidly growing economy. With prosperity came a demand for goods and craftsmen.

Salt-box houses were built in Springfield and throughout New England and occupied by farmers and craftsmen. From the exterior, the Reuben Bliss House in Springfield is a typical example of this form. The photograph of the house taken prior to its demolition in the early 1920s does not suggest the elaborate second story room with its fully wainscoted walls and ceiling. An exceedingly rare feature, this room may have been created by Bliss himself, who was a joiner—a carpenter/furniture maker.

Bliss purchased five acres and one hundred and five rods of land lying on the east side of the Town Road of Springfield from his father-in-law, Luke Hitchcock, on August 15, 1754. He paid fifty-six pounds and eleven shillings. In the deed Hitchcock described the homestead as the one "on which I now Dwell." The Bliss House was on the corner of Main and Montpelier in Springfield and probably was standing at the time of the 1754 transaction.

The son of a shoemaker from East Windsor, Connecticut, Bliss was born about 1726. During the American Revolution, he received payment for providing wooden stocks for rifles. In 1799, he drew up his will: "To my beloved son Calvin, one-half interest in my shop and store and the whole of my joiner's tools." The father of seven children, he died in 1806. He was praised in his obituary in the Springfield newspaper: "In this town Thursday last, Mr. Reuben Bliss aged 80 [died]—long respected as a useful member of society, and an exemplary professor of Christianity." For at least three generations, the Bliss family personified "that useful member of society," the craftsman.

The Bliss House was a gable-ended frame structure. Two stories faced the street, with the rear roof sweeping down from the top of the gable to one story at the back. A characteristic New England feature, this sweeping rear roof covered a room extending across the back of the house. A single chimney at the center of the house served all of the fireplaces. Although not sophisticated high-style architecture, the salt-box was a practical, vernacular form suited to New England's rugged climate.

Typically in the salt-box form access to the house was through a central entrance leading to a small space in front of a staircase winding in front of the central chimney. On the ground floor, two front rooms flanked the chimney and a long room ran behind. On the second floor, the room arrangement was the same.

In addition to his father's joining tools, Calvin Bliss inherited the family home, which he in turn bequeathed to his eldest son, Henry. Bliss descendants and others owned or occupied the house through the nineteenth century. By the twentieth century, the commercial value of the property apparently exceeded its worth as a residence. In 1922, the house or its woodwork was offered for sale by Charles Woolsey Lyon, a New York City antiques dealer. The Museum purchased the woodwork through Lyon

that year. By 1924, the house had been torn down and a garage built in its place.

The Reuben Bliss chamber now installed in The Brooklyn Museum was one of the upstairs front rooms. The plain exterior of the house did not suggest the rich interior finish of these rooms. Fully paneled rooms are unusual in New England houses, and a fully paneled ceiling even rarer. When he died Bliss left property worth one thousand pounds sterling, an estate of a comfortable craftsman. His profession as a joiner probably enabled him to indulge in the luxury of a paneled room, since he had materials on hand and would not have to pay for labor.

Whether or not the unfinished woodwork is a result of twentieth-century stripping or an eighteenth-century intention remains unclear. Although eighteenth-century pine woodwork was generally painted for aesthetic reasons, tradition has it that the Bliss room was never painted. Traces of paint or paste remnants from wallpaper or some other white

substance can be detected in the paneling throughout the woodwork, but until further research can be completed, the chamber remains unpainted.

With only a few alterations, including the reconstruction of the beam spanning the ceiling, the room from the Bliss House was opened to the public in 1929. Since that time, the room has been furnished and interpreted as a chamber. Until 1980 a high chest and matching dressing table that came from the area of Wethersfield, Connecticut, and descended in the Porter and Belden families were exhibited in the room. In 1980, because the Museum also owns two rooms from the Porter-Belden House, the two pieces were removed to those rooms.

In 1929 simple printed cotton curtains hung at the windows, and the bed was dressed in white figured dimity with ball fringe (see illustrations, pages 10 and 11). In the 1940s these simple bed and window treatments were replaced by a set of red and white English printed cotton hangings marked with

Chamber 1980 renovation PHOTOS: PAUL WARCHOL

the name of I. Jones and the date 1761 (see illustration, page 10). These hangings were removed in 1980, partly for their preservation and partly because English copperplate printed cottons and the similar French toiles de Jouy were new expensive luxury goods in the 1760s and '70s and most certainly beyond the means of a small town craftsman like Reuben Bliss.

These decisions to remove the Wethersfield furniture and the printed cotton hangings prompted a reevaluation and simplification of the room. Except among the wealthy in both town and country, curtains were luxuries and were, therefore, not used in the renovation. The floor remains uncovered as were most floors until cheap mass-produced carpeting became widely available in the mid-nineteenth century.

The objects selected for the room in 1980 make broad statements about furniture making from the late seventeenth to the end of the eighteenth century in America. The broad, low chest between the windows

Chest dated 1697, Essex County, Massachusetts; oak (Henry L. Batterman Fund, 17.9)

Above, and facing page: *1929 installation*   Below: *1940s installation*

is an example of joined work. The front of the chest, with panels set into mortised and tenoned frames secured with wooden pegs was constructed like the paneling of the room. Applied moldings typical of Essex County, Massachusetts, decorate the chest and bear slight traces of decorative paint. The foot brackets on the front of the chest bear the unidentified initials "ET" and the date 1697, possibly commemorating a marriage.

On the chest is a small box with a hinged lid and a front chip-carved in a series of arches. This box dates to the seventeenth century and was probably made in the Plymouth area of Massachusetts. It was an easily moved container for papers, books, or small objects.

The table to the left of the fireplace is of a common type made throughout New England and elsewhere in the eighteenth and early nineteenth centuries. The decoration consists of turnings on the legs which were formed on a lathe. Applied molding, fielded paneling, incised carving, and lathe turning were continuous methods used by American craftsmen working in the carpenter/joiner tradition throughout the eighteenth century.

The high chest, with its bold trumpet-turned legs, is a New England example dating between 1715 and 1740. It illustrates the difference between

Box *dated 1686*
Massachusetts; oak
(Henry L. Batterman Fund, 15.424)

High Chest
circa *1715–40*
Massachusetts
walnut veneer
(Dick S. Ramsay
Fund, 58.35)

carpenter/joiner and cabinetmaker. Dove-tailed joints in the construction of the drawers and the use of highly figured veneers show the expanding technology and specificity of craftsmanship.

The simple bed with turned corner posts is a form which changed little over several centuries. The bed is fitted out with a bed rugg, a popular rural bed covering in pre-industrial America. During the seventeenth and eighteenth centuries, the term rugg meant a bedcover, not a covering for the floor. Such ruggs were not only decorative but also an important source of warmth in houses where chambers often went unheated. This example is dated 1790 and is thought to have been made in the Norwich-New London area of Connecticut. A similar example at the Winterthur Museum, illustrated here, bears the date 1783. The foundation of Brooklyn's rugg is three lengths of vertically seamed cloth on which simple running stitches have been worked in wool in three shades of blue with white highlights. Bed ruggs were made by sewing and were not hooked.

The 1980 installation of the room from the Reuben Bliss House represents the chamber of a moderately successful village craftsman or other businessman living out of the sphere of any large urban area in a small, autonomous riverside community. In such towns architecture and furnishings reflected slowly changing tastes barely altered until the Industrial Revolution.

Bed Rugg *dated 1790*
Norwich-New London area,
Connecticut; wool
Initialed "REG"
(Museum Collection Fund, 49.189a)

Bed Rugg *dated 1783*
Norwich-New London area of
Connecticut; wool; initialed "RWB"
Collection: The Henry Francis du Pont Winterthur Museum

Chamber 1980 renovation   PHOTO: PAUL WARCHOL

The Porter-Belden House
CIRCA *1760–1800*

Wethersfield, Connecticut

Although it is now virtually a suburb of Hartford, Wethersfield, Connecticut, was a separate and prosperous community throughout the eighteenth century. Founded in the seventeenth century as one of the first towns in the

colony, it became, by virtue of its location on the Connecticut River, a busy port and a center of shipbuilding.

The eighteenth-century Porter-Belden House which still stands in greatly altered state at 400 Main Street in Wethersfield is a commodious frame dwelling, a mansion by Wethersfield standards. Two front rooms from the house have been preserved in The Brooklyn Museum, installed as a parlor and a downstairs chamber. These installations are unique in the Museum's eighteenth-century series because they contain furniture known to have been used in the original house.

Although nineteenth-century accounts refer to the location of the Porter-Belden House as the "Fort-Site," since the seventeenth century the lot has been occupied by dwellings. Thomas and Susannah Standish lived on the property until their deaths in 1692–93, and in 1743 Dr. Ezekiel Porter bought the lot for a thousand pounds in bills. Though the 1743 deed of transfer included all buildings on the property,

whatever buildings existed there at the time are unrecorded.

Traditionally, Dr. Porter, a prominent physician who actively invested in real estate, has been credited with building the house that now stands at 400 Main sometime in the 1750s. Although similar-style houses were built in the mid-eighteenth century in more urban areas of New England, such an early date seems unlikely in relation to other houses in the Wethersfield area. It may be that the house was built in the late 1790s by Frederick Butler, who married Porter's granddaughter Mary Belden in 1787. Butler inherited the Main Street lot in 1797 upon the death of Porter's widow, and in 1798 the property jumped in value to $2,000—the third highest valuation in town.

Originally, the gable-ended house had a central stairhall with two rooms on each side—a Georgian-style arrangement common in America in the second half of the eighteenth century. The facade was symmetrical and sparsely ornamented, with a dentil molding under the front eave—a

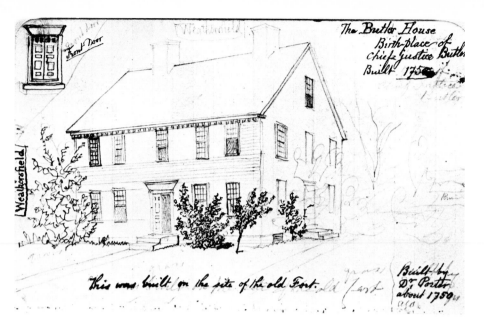

Edwin Whitefield
Porter-Belden House circa 1875
Ink and pencil on paper
Collection: The Society for the
Preservation of New England
Antiquities, Boston
Photo courtesy: Peter Benes

The backs of two chairs now in the
Museum can be seen in this 1890s
photograph of Esther Bidwell sitting in
the Porter-Belden House's parlor. Miss
Bidwell was the niece of Mary Belden,
the last Porter descendent to live in the
house.

feature uncommon in Wethersfield
until after the Revolution. A flared
pediment over the door, now lost,
appears in a nineteenth-century sketch
of the house in the Society for the
Preservation of New England
Antiquities in Boston.

Throughout the nineteenth century,
the house was occupied by members of
the Belden, Butler, and Bidwell
families, all descendents of Dr. Porter.
The final family member, also named
Mary Belden, died in 1910. Only after
her death was it disclosed that she had
secretly married an attorney named
John Parsons. He and her grandniece
Esther Allerton were involved in the
sale of the house and the distribution of
its contents. Three years before the
Museum acquired the rooms from the
house, it bought a core group of Porter-
Belden furniture from Parsons—its first
acquisition of early-American
furniture. Later, in the 1940s, additional
furnishings related to the house were
purchased from Miss Allerton.

In 1914, the year he sold the furniture
to the Museum, Parsons also sold the
property itself to Thomas McNierney,
retaining rights to occupy two rooms
rent free until June 1, 1916. It was
probably about this time that the
building was renovated into
apartments. In a letter now in the
Wethersfield Historical Society, Miss
Allerton asserted that everything of
value was removed from the house
prior to the house's sale out of the
family. The interior woodwork was sold
to Hartford antiques dealer Morris
Schwartz, from whom the Museum
purchased the two front ground floor
rooms in 1917.

Nineteenth-century photographs of
the interiors *in situ* attest to the spatial
accuracy of the Museum's
reconstructions and show furniture
that was later purchased by the
Museum. Luke Vincent Lockwood was
familiar with the house when it was
occupied by Mary Belden and her niece
Esther Bidwell in the 1890s, and
furniture from the house was included
in his 1901 book *Colonial Furniture in
America*. It was his belief that Porter
was responsible for the construction of
the house and had originally owned the
group of furniture.

The two interiors now in the
Museum were the front or "best"
rooms of the house. The rooms behind
them probably had simpler woodwork.
A passage runs between the period
rooms, suggesting the stairhall of the
original configuration. It is possible
that the rooms' positions were reversed
when they were installed.

Although many of the Museum's
eighteenth-century rooms are fully
paneled, the partial paneling in the
Porter-Belden rooms (only the
fireplace walls are fully wainscoted) is
far more typical of the period. Like the
exterior of the house, the woodwork is
conservative, if not slightly out of
fashion. Heavy fielded paneling in a
mid-eighteenth century style is
combined with Classical details in a
way that would have been outmoded in
Boston or even Hartford by the late
eighteenth century. But in smaller
towns like Wethersfield, traditions of
craftsmanship and taste continued over
a longer period of time.

When they opened in 1929, the
Porter-Belden rooms (then called the
Porter-Bidwell rooms) were shown as
two front parlors. One room,
considered a formal parlor, contained
heavy red damask drapes and high-
style Queen Anne and Chippendale
furniture of both English and American
make. The other room, depicted as a
family sitting room, was furnished
more conservatively, with simple
printed fabric curtains and Porter-
Belden heirlooms. The major
difference apart from the window
treatments and furnishings was the use
of eighteenth-century English
wallpaper in the room designated as
the better parlor. This wallpaper,
which has remained in the room, was
found in an unused condition by
Lockwood. Advertisements in colonial
newspapers indicate that wallpaper
was readily available, inexpensive, and
probably more frequently used than
has generally been recognized.
Certainly it would have been available
in a river port like Wethersfield. In fact,
it is recorded that when George
Washington visited the town in 1781 he
slept in a newly wallpapered chamber
in the Webb House. Though the

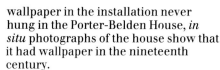

wallpaper in the installation never hung in the Porter-Belden House, *in situ* photographs of the house show that it had wallpaper in the nineteenth century.

The practice of furnishing one room as a better parlor and the other as a family sitting room was retained until the 1980 renovation with few changes in furnishings or arrangement. John Graham tested for paint colors in the 1940s, and the rooms were painted according to his findings. He found the woodwork in the parlor to have been painted a green which conveniently matched the wallpaper, and in the sitting room he found a light brown. In the 1980 renovation, these colors were again confirmed and the rooms were repainted.

In 1980 it was also decided to convert one of the rooms to a ground floor chamber (illustrated on pages 13 and 17) in order to more appropriately display two important Porter-Belden chamber case pieces—a high chest and a dressing table—that had been exhibited in the Reuben Bliss chamber from Springfield, Massachusetts, since the period rooms opened. Such ground floor chambers were often found in seventeenth- and eighteenth-century houses. Central in determining which room should be designated the chamber was the quality of the woodwork. Since the more elaborate woodwork of the "family sitting room" suggested an important public space, it was furnished as a parlor, and the former "best parlor" became the chamber.

Top: *The chamber interpreted as a more formal parlor in 1929*

Left: *The room (now the parlor) interpreted as a family sitting room in 1929*

Parlor in situ, circa *1917*

The mahogany high chest and dressing table are believed to have been owned by Dr. Porter. Their finely carved shells, cabriole legs terminating in pad feet, and skirts with accentuated curves associate them with the Queen Anne style. They were probably made in the Wethersfield/Hartford area in the third quarter of the eighteenth century. Such pieces were expensive and are an indication of the affluence of the Porter, Butler, and Belden families.

Among the other furnishings in the chamber is a blanket chest that is the earliest piece of Porter-Belden furniture in the Museum's collection. The stylized, incised floral decoration on its facade relates it to a group of chests known to have been made in the early eighteenth century in the upper Connecticut River Valley around the Hadley and Hatfield areas of Massachusetts. By tradition, the chest belonged to Dr. Porter's wife. A household inventory taken at the time of the doctor's death in 1775 lists "one old chest with one draw." Although by that time the chest would have been considered old-fashioned, its presence in the room together with more up-to-date furniture conveys a sense of practicality in retaining a usable if out-of-date piece. In the eighteenth century, like today, rooms were rarely fitted out in a single taste, but were eclectic mixes of various styles.

Four side chairs, undoubtedly from a larger set (there are five in the Museum's collection), line the walls of the room. Purchased from Esther Allerton, they are also believed to have been made locally and owned by Dr. Porter. They are painted black and have rush seats and turned legs that terminate in restrained, so-called "Spanish" or "paintbrush" feet. Although these particular features suggest that the chairs are older than the dressing table and high chest, the solid back splats and yoke crests date them to about the same period. Just as furnishings in a room tend to be eclectic, so a single piece of furniture may combine elements from a number of identifiable period styles.

The chamber's eighteenth-century bed is a Connecticut example that is now painted green but was originally painted red. It is hung in a fabric known in the eighteenth century as dimity. Although today the term refers to a sheer dress fabric, then it meant a heavy white cotton fabric woven with raised stripes. It was popular for interior decoration, and here a matching dimity is used in the simple curtains hung at the windows.

Rounding out the room's furnishings is a large easy chair made in New York in the third quarter of the eighteenth

High Chest circa *1740–75 Wethersfield/Hartford area, Conn.; mahogany and white pine (Henry L. Batterman Fund, 14.713)*

Dressing Table circa *1740–75 Wethersfield/Hartford area, Conn.; mahogany and white pine (Henry L. Batterman Fund, 14.714)*

Chamber *1980 renovation*   PHOTO: PAUL WARCHOL

Chest circa 1705–25
Vicinity of Hadley, Mass.; oak and pine
(Henry L. Batterman Fund, 14.707)

Chair circa 1740–75
(from a set of at least five)
Connecticut; painted maple (40.753)

17

century. It has a dimity slipcover secured to it with tied ribbons of the same material. Such chairs, which were used in chambers but not in more formal rooms, were intended for napping and convalescing.

The other Porter-Belden room now represents a well-ordered eighteenth-century New England parlor (see illustrations on pages 20–21). There is no sofa or settee, for even in the last half of the eighteenth century such items rarely appeared in American inventories and rooms seem to have been furnished largely with chairs. Except for the lolling chair and table that have been drawn before the fireplace as if for a solitary light meal, the furniture lines the perimeter of the room. The presence of the lolling chair, a Rhode Island example dating to about 1800, suggests a certain relaxation in furniture forms for more formal rooms.

Like four other chairs in the room, the lolling chair has a slipcover of blue furniture check. Slipcovers, called loose cases or simply cases in the eighteenth century, were used by virtually everyone wealthy enough to own upholstered furniture. Such furniture was often equipped with loose covers at the time of manufacture, and costly upholstery probably only saw the light of day on the rarest and most important occasions. Slipcovers made of linen in checks of all sizes and colors are documented in both written and pictorial sources (see below).

Three side chairs have seats which are covered in needlework. Decorative embroidery in variants of Florentine needlepoint was very popular among the wealthy in the seventeenth and eighteenth centuries. It was an expensive hobby because the wools and canvas could not be produced at home. Ladies took lessons in the arts of plain and fancy needlework, and it was the mark of a gentlewoman to be able to execute work like that on these chairs. The reproductions shown here copy the combination of flame and carnation patterns worked into the wool-on-coarse-canvas originals.

These chairs were used in the Porter-Belden house through the nineteenth century. Curved seats, cabriole legs, and solid back splats identify them with the Queen Anne style and probably date them to about the same time as the case pieces in the chamber: the third quarter of the eighteenth century. Part of a much larger set, these chairs are identical to ones now in the Yale University Art Gallery and the Museum of Fine Arts in Boston. The Yale example is inscribed with the initials "AP," perhaps for Dr. Porter's daughter Abigail.

The fall-front desk-on-frame between the windows, with its cabriole legs and carved shells, relates to the Porter-Belden furniture and, like that group, was probably made in the area.

John Hamilton Mortimer
Sergeant at Arms Bonfoy, his son (?), and John Clementson, Sr.
circa 1760
Oil on canvas
Collection: Yale Center for British Art
(Paul Mellon Collection)

Chair *circa 1740–75*
(one of three)
Connecticut; cherry
(Henry L. Batterman Fund, 14.710)

Desk *circa 1740–75*
Hartford, Conn.; mahogany
(Dick S. Ramsay Fund, 64.87)

Parlor *1980 renovation*   PHOTOS: PAUL WARCHOL

It was originally owned by Nathaniel Brown of Hartford.

The tall clock in the corner was made about 1800 by Simon Willard of Roxbury, Massachusetts. Although clocks were luxury items in the eighteenth century, they became more common as the clockmaking industry began to flourish throughout New England at the beginning of the Industrial Revolution.

Set on the portable tilt-top tea table is a small teapot dating to the 1760s—an example of the mass-produced English pottery that was widely available to American colonists and continued to dominate the American market well into the nineteenth century. The pot is made of cream-colored earthenware and is decorated with a scene transferred from an engraved copper plate. The molded wall pockets or vases

hanging above the fireplace are also of English manufacture.

From the blanket chest in the chamber to the tall clock in the parlor, the furnishings in the Porter-Belden rooms span a century of craftsmanship and taste. They appear to have been put together more by chance than by intent. As a result, the rooms from the Porter-Belden House suggest continuous occupancy by an affluent and conservative family over several generations.

Right:
Teapot *1760–70*
Possibly Leeds, England; creamware
(Gift of Reverend Alfred Duane Pell,
03.328.206)

Far right:
Wall Pockets *circa 1775*
England; lead-glazed earthenware
(H. Randolph Lever Fund, 67.18.1–2)

The Russell House
CIRCA 1772

Providence, Rhode Island

By the 1770s, Providence, Rhode Island, was surpassing Newport as the major commercial center of the colony. Two merchants, the brothers Joseph and William Russell, built a commodious brick mansion on King (now Main) Street around 1772. The house reflected the demand for high quality design by citizens made affluent during the town's economic growth. The wood work from the northeast parlor of this house is the most sophisticated and finely crafted in the Museum's eighteenth-century period rooms.

Above: *Front door*

Right: *Design plate*
from The Builders' Compleat Assistant *by Batty Langley, 2nd ed., London, 1738*

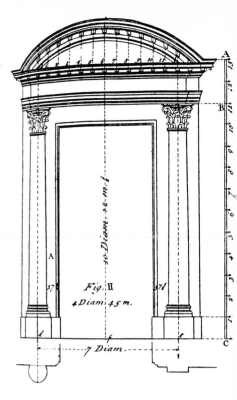

In 1759, the Russells purchased half the lot on which they would build the house and in 1771 they secured the remaining half. On King Street the lot backed onto a channel which led to the

Providence River. With its easy access to water transportation, the site was prime real estate in the eighteenth century. In their mercantile rooms near the court house the brothers dealt in imported goods including ceramics, glass, cheese, and liquor.

The exterior of the square brick mansion, which is still standing, is restrained and conservative. Three bands of brick horizontal stringing delineate the three floors, and a dentil molding runs under the eave of a hipped roof which is capped by a monitor and lantern that may or may not be original.

The entrance at the center of the five-bay facade is the most elaborate ornament on the exterior of the house. It consists of a demi-luned pediment with crisply carved dentils supported by a pair of Corinthian columns. The direct source for the treatment seems to be a design plate in Batty Langley's *Builders' Compleat Assistant,* second edition, published in London in 1738. In its restraint the house is similar to the houses of affluent English merchants seen in towns and cities all over Britain.

Throughout the eighteenth century English designers published architectural pattern books. These pattern books were illustrated with suggested designs for architectural details, including door surrounds and fireplaces. They were widely circulated throughout the American colonies, and the anonymous builder of the Russell House relied heavily on them.

Exterior of the Russell House circa *1950*

In 1800 the Russell property passed [out] of the family to John Corliss, [an]other merchant, apparently to settle [de]bts owed by the Russell business. [O]ver the next one hundred and twenty [ye]ars the house was owned by a [nu]mber of individuals and used for a [va]riety of purposes. At some point in [th]e nineteenth century the house was [ei]ther elevated or the grade of the [st]reet lowered, and the entrace to the [ho]use is now on the second story of a [co]mmercial building (see photograph [of] exterior on p. 22). In the early [tw]entieth century, the structure was [kn]own as the Clarendon Hotel.

[E]rnest Blazar and Samuel Joseph [ow]ned the property in 1920 when the [in]terior woodwork was removed from [th]e house. The Brooklyn Museum [pu]rchased the two front rooms and the [ce]ntral stairhall between them, and a [Pr]ovidence dealer purchased the two [ro]oms directly above (these are now at [th]e Denver Art Museum). Andre Rueff [w]as called in to supervise the removal [of] the woodwork, coding the elements [by] numbering the panels and taking [ph]otographs to guide reconstruction [w]ithin the Museum.

[A]lthough no local efforts at [p]reserving the Russell House intact are [k]nown, one local reporter expressed [h]is outrage at representatives from The [B]rooklyn Museum and The [M]etropolitan Museum of Art in New [Y]ork who "highly valued the prize, and [w]ere only waiting for an opportunity to [ob]tain it." His anger was apparent [w]hen he continued his story:

"It so happened that a representative of The Brooklyn Museum ascertained that the Clarendon Hotel was soon to be dismantled in part, and before the local admirers and coveters of the cherished woodwork

Northeast parlor of the Russell House *in situ, circa 1920. This is the room now installed at The Brooklyn Museum.*

could circumvent him he had purchased the finish of the best two rooms in the house and taken it to Brooklyn. He had been after those two rooms and part of the staircase for four years and by patient waiting and quiet campaigning succeeded in his endeavor."

Whether the Providence journalist was referring to Rueff, who actually removed the paneling, or to Luke Vincent Lockwood, who negotiated its sale to the Museum, is unknown.

In his overall Museum scheme, Lockwood may have planned to install the two Russell rooms on either side of the central stairhall, imitating the

original arrangement as he did in the Southern rooms. However, within two years the simpler of the front two rooms was sold to The Minneapolis Institute of Arts, where it was installed in slightly larger form in 1924. In 1929 the Brooklyn room was installed, and in the 1940s the central stairhall was transferred to The Denver Art Museum.

Below, left:
*Installation of the **southeast parlor** of the Russell House at The Minneapolis Institute of Arts*

Below: ***Stairhall*** *of the Russell House in situ. The hall is now installed in The Denver Art Museum.*

The fireplace wall of the Russell room is the most academic of all the interior architecture in the Museum's rooms, following strict rules of architectural order. With an emphasis on symmetry, the two niches flank a temple-form fireplace. Thus a grand Italian Rennaissance concept for a stone public facade is turned inward for a fireplace wall in wood in an eighteenth-century Rhode Island interior. The fireplace opening is flanked by columns with scrolled Ionic capitals. In classic Rennaissance manner more delicate Corinthian capitals top the pilasters in the over-mantle. The light forms over the heavy tend to draw the eye to the triangular dentilled pediment at the top.

The niches which flank the fireplace can also be traced to Classical sources. In grand European buildings such niches housed sculpture or other works of art. Here, in an eighteenth-century Rhode Island room, the niches provide seating and contribute to the overall

The Russell parlor *1980 renovation*

Plate from William Salmon's Palladio Londonensis, *London, 1748*

Elevation of the mantel wall
in the Museum's Cupola House hall

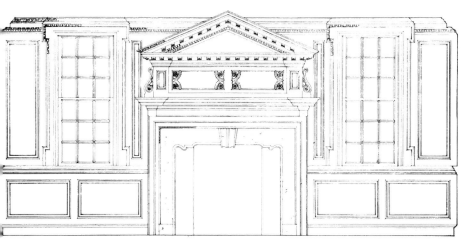

balance. A sense of depth in the niches is accomplished by their arched ceilings' downward slant, which lends greater perspective to a small space. This subtle detail attests to the skill of the designer/craftsman. Even the paint color, a stone putty, reflects an understanding of Renaissance ideas which were often translated into stone.

The inspiration for the fireplace itself seems to have been a design in William Salmon's *Palladio Londonensis,* which was published in 1748 and was a frequently consulted source for architectural details. The same source or memory thereof seems to have provided inspiration to the designer and builder of the fireplace wall in the Museum's Cupola House hall from Edenton, North Carolina. But the result in Edenton lacks subtlety and understanding of the classical rules of architecture. In the Russell parlor, the scale of each element in relation to one another and to the overall space makes for one of the architecturally most

1980 renovation   PHOTOS: PAUL WARCHOL

The Russell parlor 1929 installation

1950s installation

1970s installation

successful rooms to survive from eighteenth-century America.

In 1929 the room from the Russell House was presented as a parlor, reception, or entertainment room. Since the chairs that were placed around the walls would have suggested a room not in use in the eighteenth century, the opened tea table that was placed in the center would have been out of place. While center tables were fashionable in the nineteenth century, eighteenth-century folding tea tables were designed to be set unobtrusively against the wall when not in use. The windows were hung in heavy blue silk damask draperies and valances, a treatment more popular in the early twentieth century than it was in the 1700s.

In the 1950s Marvin Schwartz, consulting with designer Victor Proetz (who designed the Museum's nineteenth-century period room installations in the 1950s), renovated the room. Paint research revealed the original putty color. High-style eighteenth-century New England furniture which had long been on loan to the Museum furnished the room. Swag drapes in a bright English chintz pattern based on Indian designs were placed at the windows.

In 1970 the room was presented with lively details suggesting bustling activity. A desk arranged for writing, a fully set tea table, and a card game in progress portrayed a variety of pursuits. A male mannequin in eighteenth-century dress was placed in the room in an attempt to give it human warmth.

The 1980 decision to present the Russell room unoccupied and not in

Side Chair circa 1740-60
Rhode Island; walnut
(Bequest of Mrs. William
Sterling Peters 50.141.2)

use was based on three considerations. The nature of the Museum's permanent holdings made an appropriate and complete furnishing impossible. Furnishing the room sparsely placed greater emphasis on its architecture and conveyed an eighteenth-century sense of room and furniture usage.

In the eighteenth century, rooms were used for a wide variety of purposes. The Russell room could have been used for entertaining, receiving, dining, or business. Such activities required different objects, and furniture was moved from room to room or even house to house as seasons changed. The twentieth-century sense of permanence—a table in the dining room or a sofa in the living room—was not familiar to the eighteenth-century concept of everyday life.

Three chairs are shown in the room: a pair flanking the door and a single chair by the opposite wall. All three are in the Queen Anne style and date to around 1750. Characteristic of this style are repeated curves, seen here in the S-shaped or cabriole legs and the curved fronts of the seats. The splats, panels extending from the back of the seat to the crest of the back, are vaguely vase-shaped and solid with no carved detail. The front legs of the single chair against the wall terminate in circular pad feet, a detail frequently found on furniture of the period. On the pair of chairs flanking the door, the front feet are carved in the shape of a claw clutching a ball. Although this detail is often associated with the slightly later Chippendale period, in this case it may simply be a more expensive option.

The carved shell decorating the crest of the chair by the wall is a type often found on Rhode Island and especially Newport chairs, and the chair's tall and narrow proportions further a Rhode Island attribution. Although the chairs by the door also have crests embellished by carved shells, the character of the shell and of the carved floral decoration surrounding it, as well as the chairs' low and broad stance, associate them with known New York furniture. Decorative elements were not necessarily executed in a single area, nor did furniture always stay in its city of origin. The New York chairs descended in the prominent and wealthy Bromfield family of Boston, Massachusetts.

Many eighteenth-century English paintings attest to the practice of

Side Chairs circa 1750
New York; walnut and walnut veneer
(H. Randolph Lever Fund 68.182.1-2)
These two chairs are from a set of six
and have their original needlepoint
upholstery.

placing large oriental porcelain pots in unused fireplaces, particularly during the summer. This practice probably dates from the late seventeenth century when Chinese and Japanese porcelains first became widely available in Europe and when the ornamental use of Oriental porcelains became almost a mania. About 1700 Daniel Marot, the important Huguenot designer, published engravings showing ways in which porcelains could be arranged for the decoration of interiors, and one of his solutions was the placing of pots in the fireplace. Although it is unclear whether Marot originated this convention, the practice is documented in such English genre paintings of the period as Arthur Devis's *Portrait of Mr. and Mrs. Hill.* The sophistication of the woodwork in the Russell room makes this stylish decoration appropriate. Made in China for the Western market, the urn, with its inverted pear shape, echoes the S-shaped curves of the American chairs.

Although eighteenth-century paintings often provide useful information about appropriate furnishings and fabrics, the fabric on upholstered furniture in portraits is frequently mistaken for silk. Due to its expense and fragility, silk was rarely used for upholstery except among the very wealthy. More often, fine wool worsteds or combinations of wool and silk were utilized.

A rare useage of silk is documented in the papers of John Cadwalader, who decorated his town house in Philadelphia in 1770. To suggest the wealth and sophistication of the Russells, a small amount of silk has been used for the cushions on the window seats and in the niches. No curtains are at the windows because shutters fold out from the sides providing privacy as well as warmth. By leaving the windows bare, the rarity of silk in eighteenth-century America is further emphasized. In the Museum's eighteenth-century rooms, only the Russell parlor contains any silk furnishings.

The beautifully executed and carefully ordered woodwork as well as the expensive furnishings in the Russell room provide a glimpse at the taste of the most affluent and sophisticated colonists on the eve of the Revolution.

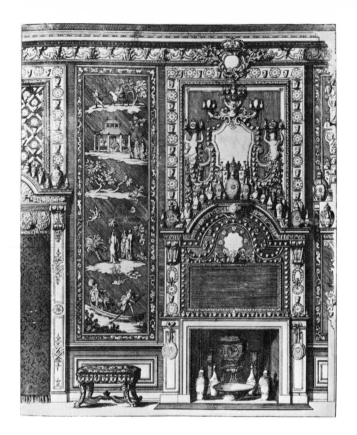

Above:
Plate from Werken Van Daniel Marot (1663-1752), Opperboumeester Van, Zyne Maiesteit, Willem Den Derden *Collection: Cooper-Hewitt Museum, The Smithsonian Institution's National Museum of Design*

Below:
Arthur Devis
Portrait of Mr. and Mrs. Hill n.d.
Oil on canvas
Collection: The Yale Center for British Art
(Paul Mellon Collection)

The Henry Trippe House
CIRCA *1724–1731*

Secretary, Maryland

Major Henry Trippe, a gentleman landowner and planter, built his one-and-a-half story brick manor house between 1724 and 1731 on a plantation called Carthagena that he had inherited from his father. The house, which is still standing, faces the head of Secretary Creek in Dorchester County

Exterior of the Trippe House *circa* 1917

***Hall** 1980 renovation*   PHOTO: PAUL WARCHOL

on Maryland's eastern shore. Its original ground floor, which is now installed in the Museum, contains the second oldest rooms in the Museum's series and provides an important early example of the use of elaborate paneling.

The Trippe family was prominent in the affairs of the colony. Major Trippe's grandfather, Lt. Col. Henry Trippe, settled at "Sark," a tract in Dorchester County, sometime in the 1660s. He served in the upper house of the Colonial Assembly and was one of the first Dorchester County Commissioners.

His eldest son, also named Henry, purchased Carthagena from "Mary Barrett of the City of London Widdow" in 1720. This second Henry Trippe died in 1723, leaving his wife, Susannah, a third of his personal estate as well as the right "to live on his now dwelling plantation during her widowhood." An indication of his prominence and wealth is the bequest of five pounds that he made to the local parish for the purchase of plate (silver). As the eldest son, Major Trippe inherited Carthagena.

The gable-ended manor house constructed by Major Trippe is typical of a number built by gentlemen planters in Maryland and Virginia during the first half of the eighteenth century. Its symmetrical facade has a central door flanked by a window on each side, and its roof has three gabled dormers projecting from both sides. The building is oriented toward the creek because in the eighteenth century the major access to it was by water. A brick hyphen, or connector, originally linked one end of the house to a detached frame kitchen, but these structures had long since disappeared by the time the Museum acquired the woodwork from the house.

In contrast to the symmetrical exterior, the interior was broken up into rooms of various sizes. Through the main entrance was a large room known as a hall which extended from the front to the back and took up just over half the first floor. The remainder of the floor was divided roughly in half; the front was a stairhall, the rear a chamber. The entire main floor was fully wainscoted with fielded paneling. On the second floor were three sleeping chambers, one above the ground floor chamber and two above the hall.

When Major Trippe died in 1744, the property passed to his eldest son Henry, who in turn bequeathed it to his nephew Henry Dickinson. John Hudson purchased the property from the Dickinson family in 1842, and over the next few decades it was sold several

times. A rendering of the manor house dating to about 1870 shows a prosperous and well-maintained country home, but toward the end of the century some of the surrounding land was sold off as the town of Secretary developed around the manor. In 1886 the property was purchased by Joseph Cook and Joseph Conkle, and in 1917 Mrs. Conkle negotiated the sale of the house's ground floor woodwork to The Brooklyn Museum. Nine years later the property was sold to the Roman Catholic Diocese of Wilmington, Delaware, and the house now survives in altered form as the rectory for the neighboring Catholic church.

Until as recently as 1969, Major Trippe's manor house was generally believed to have been built by Nicholas

This photograph of a watercolor of the Trippe House painted about 1870, at the time the property was owned by Alward Johnson, was given to the Museum in 1925 by Johnson's daughter, Mrs. A. B. Casselman.

Hall fireplace in situ, circa *1917*

Temporary installation of the hall in 1923

ewall or his descendents. Sewall, who was secretary to the governor of the olony, Lord Baltimore, was awarded a rge tract of property in 1664 on the pposite side of Secretary Creek. ecause he was also presumed to have wned the property on which the anor house stood, the house was ought to date to the late seventeenth entury. These mistaken assumptions ere challenged by Esther Sard Dorsey nd Sylvia Kemp Sard in their book *The eritage of Secretary in Dorchester ounty, Maryland* (Tercentenary of orchester County, 1969). Their esearch, which was confirmed and xpanded by Brooklyn Museum Mellon ellow Wendy A. Cooper in 1971, efuted any connection with Sewall and stablished the ownership of the roperty by the Trippes.

The hall (illustrated on page 29) is e largest room from the house. An all-urpose room, it was used for most aily activities, including dining, ntertaining, sleeping, and conducting usiness. At each end is a door and a indow fitted out with a bench.

Although old-fashioned by London standards, the paneling is extremely sophisticated for its time and place: heavy moldings identify its style as American William and Mary. The large fireplace is surrounded by a bolection molding, and the ceiling has a bold cornice which although a 1929 fabrication is in keeping with the original woodwork. The closets flanking the fireplace are an architectural feature of early eighteenth-century houses in the Tidewater area of Maryland and Virginia. They often had windows and were probably used for storage.

Close examination of the paneling on the fireplace wall reveals early changes. There is definite evidence of fire damage, and it is clear that the paneling was reorganized sometime in the eighteenth century. The scallop-topped doors of the closets may have been added after the house was built, and the original windows and exterior doors were replaced in the early nineteenth century. Furthermore, since the fireplace has bolection molding, it is unlikely that the mantle shelf that

was in place when the Museum acquired the woodwork is original. When the room was temporarily set up in 1923, this small shelf or a reproduction of it was utilized. A boldly molded shelf that was fabricated to replace it in 1929 remained in place until 1980, when, since there was no documentation for any other shelf over the fireplace, the small shelf was reproduced from a 1917 *in situ* photograph.

The temporary installation of the house in 1923 is documented both by photographs and by an article that Luke Vincent Lockwood wrote for *The Brooklyn Museum Quarterly* in July of that year. Although no paint research was done for this first installation, the rooms were painted white with black trim. These colors were appropriate for the 1920s, but were rare, if not unknown, in the eighteenth century.

In his article, Lockwood described the sources he had used in planning the installation: probate records, wills, inventories, contemporary letters, diaries, and newspapers, as well as

1923 installation

1929 installation

1929 installation

books on manners and customs, both English and American. Fifty years later modern scholarship still depends on these same sources.

Lockwood's arrangement of the furniture in the hall was successful in conveying an eighteenth-century look. The room was uncluttered, and, except for a table in the center of the room, the furniture lined the walls. Noting that "a carpet at this time was never used for floor covering, and up to the middle of the eighteenth century floors were not covered," Lockwood correctly placed a carpet on the table.

In the fifty years after this initial installation, the hall underwent various transformations as taste and scholarship changed. The room became more richly furnished, and heavy velvet, and, later, green brocade, curtains with elaborate trim were hung at the windows. Flat cushions were placed on the window seats, and, despite Lockwood's 1923 statements, by 1929 Oriental carpets were placed on the floor. The furniture was rearranged in the center of the room, conveying the look of a nineteenth-century parlor rather than that of an eighteenth-century hall.

In the 1940s, John Graham conducted scrapings of the paint to determine the earliest color. He found what he thought was a light brown, and the room was painted accordingly. At the beginning of the 1980 renovation, further paint analysis revealed that the room had been painted twice in the eighteenth century and apparently never in the nineteenth century. These two eighteenth-century colors were an original coat of yellow ochre, which Graham had probably mistaken for brown, and a second coat of gray. Because the adjoining chamber had been painted yellow ochre since the 1940s, it seemed that the opportunity should be taken to show another early eighteenth-century color scheme—in this case, gray—in the hall. Gray, a popular color, was sometimes called "stone" in eighteenth-century written sources, and it was in fact intended to give wooden paneling a stone-like quality.

The room is now furnished as if not in use. Chairs line the walls, and a large drop-leaf table is placed out of the way

1940s installations

1980 renovation

and covered with an Oriental carpet. That Oriental carpets were owned by wealthy Americans is illustrated in Robert Feke's 1741 portrait of the Isaac Royall family.

The furniture is in the William and Mary and early Queen Anne styles and is of American and English manufacture. Turned decoration on furniture legs and the use of stepped or scalloped arches are salient characteristics of these styles. In fact, the scalloped or stepped arch is seen throughout the room. The crests of the chairs, the back of the couch, the japanned English mirror hanging over the table, the skirt of the slate-topped mixing table, and the closet doors flanking the fireplace—all express this popular Baroque motif.

The three English walnut side chairs and matching armchair, which date to between 1690 and 1710, all have cane seats and backs and are fitted with blue wool cushions called squabs. Seventeenth- and eighteenth-century probate inventories indicate widespread use of cushions of this kind, and English, Scandinavian, and Dutch pictures of the period often show loose pillows for the seats of furniture. Chairs with cane seats were meant to be used with cushions, since the cane served as a springy platform. Upholstery records show that these cushions sometimes contained a pound and a half of feathers. They were expensive, and their use on these chairs, as well as on the window seats and couch, indicates a desire for luxury and comfort.

The couch, a kind of bed with a reclining back, is maple and has turned legs and stretchers. Probably made in

Left:
Plate from Dend hyrdinde Astrea
by Soren Terkelsen (Copenhagen, 1645),
documenting the early European
use of squabs
Collection: The Royal Library
Copenhagen

Below:
Couch 1700-30
Boston; maple
(Henry L. Batterman Fund, 15.481)

Boston, it dates to between 1700 and 1730.

The mixing table, probably made between 1710 and 1730, has a veneered walnut base. The top comprises a slab of slate surrounded by an elaborate marquetry frame whose decoration of stylized lions and floral motifs expresses the period taste for rich pattern. Although this top was probably made in Switzerland, the heavy trumpet-turned legs and symmetrical cross-stretcher identify the base with a sophisticated American interpretation of the William and Mary style. The bottom of the table was undoubtedly made in an urban area, either New York or Boston, specifically to accommodate the elaborate top, which was practical for mixing beverages or serving hot dishes. Owning a table fitted out for such specific purposes was a luxury unavailable to most Americans.

Interest in rich textures and color is further conveyed in the pair of quillwork sconces which flank the fireplace. These shadow boxes were filled with bits of paper wrapped around quills and assembled to form floral shapes. The assembled arrangements in the boxes were then sprinkled with bits of mica. When the candles were lit, the effect was one of sparkling depth. The silver candle brackets on this pair were provided by Knight Leverett of Boston, who was active between 1703 and 1753, and the quillwork was done by Ruth Read of Boston about 1720. In the 1740s, advertisements often appeared in colonial newspapers offering quillwork lessons to young ladies of fashion.

Prints of portraits, religious subjects, and old master paintings were favorite wall decorations in eighteenth-century American homes. Often they were simply tacked to the wall, but in houses of the wealthy they were generally framed in a combination of black wood and gilt. Given the emphasis on symmetry in this period, it is surprising that there was sometimes little regard for balance in the hanging of pictures. Haphazard arrangements are clearly documented in contemporary English interior views.

The window curtains are hung in a simple style prevalent in America before 1750. They are knotted as they would have been to keep them from blowing about when the windows were opened. Although they look quite short to our contemporary eyes in this position, it must be remembered that fabric was an imported luxury and therefore expensive. To economize, the curtains were cut so that when they were unknotted they just filled the space of the window. The modern printed cotton, or chintz, used here is a

Above:
Mixing Table 1710-30
America; walnut veneer with
Continental marquetry and slate top
(Henry L. Batterman Fund, 15.33)

Right:
Wall Sconce circa 1720
(one of a pair)
Made by Ruth Read, Boston;
quillwork, silver, glass,
and black painted frame.
Silver candle brackets by
Knight Leverett, Boston
(active 1703-53)
Collection: Cooper-Hewitt Museum,
The Smithsonian Institution's
National Museum of Design,
L80.18.2

Facing page:
Stair passage 1980 renovation
PHOTO: PAUL WARCHOL

large overall pattern of the type popular during the early eighteenth century. In seventeenth-century America the term chintz, or calico, had referred to printed or painted fabrics imported from India by way of England. By the eighteenth century, however, Europeans were able to manufacture chintz themselves, and printed cotton textiles became a significant part of interior decoration in both Europe and America.

The stair passage off the hall provides access to the downstairs chamber as well as to a side door,

Stair passage ceiling before 1980 renovation   *Built-in cupboard* stair passage

which at one time led to the detached kitchen. The staircase itself is a triple run with two landings. In 1929, the ceiling of the stairwell was simply boxed in, giving no indication of how this space had looked in the house. In the 1980 renovation, a dormer, which in the original house provided light for the staircase, was recreated, and the ceiling was slanted to indicate the pitch of the roof.

Research on the paint in the stairhall revealed that the paneling and the staircase had been stripped. Since it was impossible to determine the original color, the stone gray in the hall was utilized here as well.

Because the public has access to this area, the passage has no furnishings. However, there are indications that it was a much-used space in the eighteenth century. Behind the door leading to the hall is a built-in cupboard fitted with compartments that were probably used for the storage of documents. Furthermore, the 1744 household inventory taken at the time

of Trippe's death lists a number of furnishings including "1 Oval Table of Cherry Tree . . . 1 Desk and Stand . . . 1 Woolen Carpet . . . 1 Cane Close Bucket . . . 1 Warm Pan." The passage may have been used for conducting business or any number of daily activities.

The small room off the stairhall is shown as a chamber (see illustration on page 40). Its corner fireplace, which has heavy bolection molding similar to the molding on the fireplace in the hall, is a convention often used in Baroque architecture. The window seat is fitted with an overstuffed squab.

In the 1940s John Graham determined that the original colors in this room had been bright ochre with red trim, and the room was painted accordingly. Initial examinations during the 1980 renovation found a verdigris green that appeared to be the earliest coat of paint. Verdigris, which was an especially expensive pigment, presents problems in reproduction because of its tendency to darken

heavily as it ages. Since a second attempt at paint analysis substantiated the red found by Graham and showed that beneath the verdigris were two coats of ochre, the room was repainted in those colors.

The arched crest and turned maple legs of the leather-upholstered chair associate it with the William and Mary style. Chairs of this type were very common and were often purchased in large sets. They were made in the Boston area in large quantities for export to other colonies. In fact, Boston was so well known for this kind of chair that advertisements and inventories of the period often refer to "Boston chairs."

The room is dominated by the bedstead and its hangings. In the eighteenth century the word bed referred to the mattress, and the frame was known as the bedstead. Bedsteads, even if elaborately made by the best cabinetmakers, were usually not very expensive. The bed and the bed-hangings, however, were among the most valuable household goods. The tradition of costly bed-hangings had originated in European palaces, where it was not uncommon for nobility to receive guests while in bed. With the growth of the middle classes in the eighteenth century, beds became an important symbol of status on both sides of the Atlantic.

Although in England and France bed-hangings were often of silk and velvet, in America the majority of hangings were made of wool, cotton, or linen. The bed-hangings in the Trippe chamber are based on a valance in the collection of The Essex Institute in Salem, Massachusetts. This valance was no doubt part of a complete set of hangings which have been lost. A full set would have consisted of head curtains, foot curtains, a head cloth, a valance, a base (what is now called a skirt), and a coverlet. Such sets were often imported to the colonies fully fabricated, and the Essex valance seems to have been made in England and brought to America in the 1720s. Bed-hangings of this quality were made by highly trained upholsterers.

Top:
Bed Valance (detail) circa 1725
England; linen warp and woolen weft, watered, waived, and figured, bound and decorated with braid, and lined with buckram
Collection: The Essex Institute, Salem, Massachusetts

Above:
William Hogarth
Marriage à la Mode IV:
The Countess's Morning Levée
circa 1743
Oil on canvas
Collection: National Gallery, London

Left:
Chair 1720-50
Boston; maple with leather upholstery
(Henry L. Batterman Fund, 15.426)

39

***Chamber** 1980 renovation*   PHOTO: PAUL WARCHOL

The Essex Institute valance is made of striped green-and-orange wool moreen embossed with a vermicelli pattern. Wool moreen is a hard, finely woven wool which is seldom made today but was very popular throughout the eighteenth century. Embossing is a process by which a decorative pattern is stamped onto a fabric to create an overall design, giving the effect of a damask at a fraction of the cost. Since no curtains exist for The Essex Institute valance, the curtains for the Trippe bed are based loosely on the bed-hangings in Hogarth's *Marriage a la Mode* (illustrated on page 39). As the most decorated part of the bed, the valance is trimmed with expensive braid trimmings. Its shaped outline and the decorative design of the trimmings clearly show the influence of Baroque symmetry.

The simple window curtains and window seat cushion match the bed-hangings. This *en suite* color scheme was considered the most appropriate and stylish treatment throughout the eighteenth century.

In the 1980 renovation of the Trippe House, the Museum tried to adhere to the inventory of the house that was taken at the time of Major Trippe's death in 1744. While they are useful tools of research, such estate inventories often raise more questions than they answer. Listed in the inventory of the hall, for instance, are "1 dozen chairs leather Bottom'd, 1 leather Couch walnut frame, 2 Arm'd Chairs leather bottoms, 2 Side Board Tables, 1 Looking Glass and Sconces, and 6 large Pictures with gilt frames." How all these objects were originally arranged in the hall or whether or not they were simply brought to the room for the convenience of the inventory clerks is impossible to determine. Still,

the inventory reveals that Trippe was a man of considerable wealth and refinement who was also able to afford quantities of plate (silver) and a library of fifty books. Accordingly, the rooms have been furnished to suggest the house of a successful planter.

The Cupola House 1976

Map of "North America From the French of Mr. D'Anville Improved with the Back Settlements of Virginia and Course of Ohio illustrated with Geographical and Historical Remarks." Published May, 1755, by the royal geographer Thomas Jeffreys. (H. Randolph Lever Fund, 78.38)

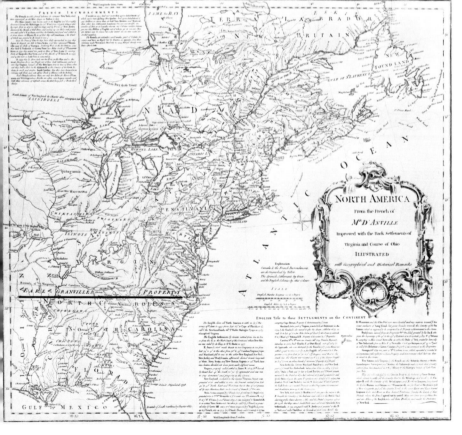

The Cupola House

CIRCA *1725*

(Woodwork 1756–58)

Edenton, North Carolina

Overlooking Albemarle Sound, Edenton in Chowan County, North Carolina, was a bustling port in the eighteenth century. Prior to the Revolution, it was one of the major towns of the colony, at times serving as the governmental seat. The largest and most impressive eighteenth-century house to survive in Edenton is the Cupola House. Located on Broad Street, the town's major thoroughfare leading to the sound, the house faces the water. Its original ground floor is now installed in The Brooklyn Museum.

Initial exploration and settlement began in the area of Edenton as early as the 1650s. The village that developed there was known as "ye town on Queen Anne's Creek" until 1722. After the death of Governor Charles Eden in that year, the town was named in his honor, and a new plan for the village was drawn up. Lot number one in this plan, the site of the Cupola House, was granted to John Lovick with the provision that he construct a house within two years. In the ensuing four years, the property changed hands a number of times, but no mention of a house or building on the site is made in any of the deeds of transfer. The earliest reference to a house on the property is in the 1726 deed from Richard Sanderson to John Dunston. A year later Dunston's widow sold the property back to Sanderson, and over the next thirty years the property was sold several times.

In 1756 the lot was purchased by Frances Corbin, who had probably come to North Carolina in the 1740s. Corbin served as land agent for Earl Granville of England, who owned large tracts in the colony, and he negotiated the sale of present-day Winston-Salem to the Moravians, a transaction that supposedly took place in the Cupola House. In his various dealings, he accumulated great wealth and even

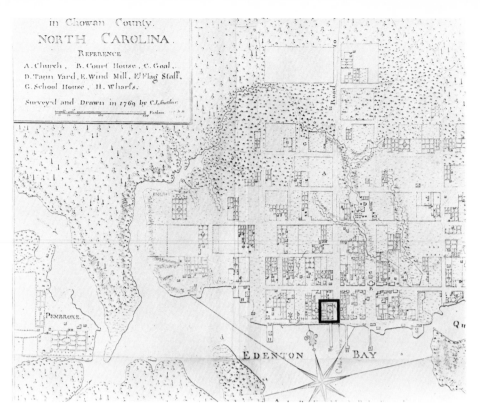

greater notoriety. Although he is believed to have sold the same property to several buyers, gaining an unseemly reputation among his fellow colonists, this did not stop him from being active in the colony's government and serving on the Governor's Council.

Two years after Corbin purchased the property he was granted the water lot adjacent to the house with the provision that he improve it, and by 1769, according to a map of the town from that year, there was a pier in front of the property. A carved finial on the front gable of the house bears the initials "FC" and the date 1758. The leaf carving on the finial relates to decorative brackets under the eaves of the main roof and the roof of the cupola crowning the house as well as to the interior woodwork. After Corbin's death in 1768, lots in Edenton belonging to him were sold to pay a debt of more than two hundred pounds that he owed to a carpenter named Robert Kirshaw. From this evidence, it is assumed that Corbin was responsible for exterior embellishments to the house, most noticeably the cupola which gives the house its name, as well as the interior woodwork which survives in the Museum.

The Cupola House has a second story that overhangs the first across the facade, the only known Southern example of this peculiarly New England type of construction. The feature has led to speculation that the

*Map of **Edenton** North Carolina, surveyed and drawn in 1769 by C. J. Sauthier. The black square indicates the location of the Cupola House.*

original structure was built between 1724 and 1726 by Richard Sanderson, who is believed to have been from New England.

The cupola on the roof of the house gives the building an eccentric Palladian appearance, and the plan of the interior is an ill-fitting attempt at Palladian balance with a central through stairhall and two rooms on either side. The flanking rooms are of unequal size, and the woodwork throughout, including the staircase, does not quite fit. These factors lead to the conclusion that the woodwork was installed in an existing structure.

After Corbin's death, the building passed to his brother Edmund, and in 1777 the property was purchased by Samuel Dickinson, an Edenton doctor. Through the nineteenth century Dickenson's descendants continued to dwell in the house. But as the population of North Carolina moved westward, and the importance of Edenton dwindled as a political and commercial center, the family found itself unable to maintain the structure.

Miss Tilly Bond, the last descendant of Dickinson to occupy the building, operated it as a boardinghouse. Despite its run-down condition, the house was known locally and to some antique dealers for its elaborate interiors. Miss Bond enjoyed showing the rooms to visitors and maintained a guest book which survives in the house today. Among the last entries in the book is the 1918 signature of Andre Rueff of The Brooklyn Museum.

A short time after Rueff's visit, the Museum bought the downstairs woodwork—an event which immediately spurred the citizens of the town to purchase the structure while the upstairs paneling and the staircase were still intact. To work for the preservation of the structure, The

The Cupola House circa *1918*

Hall in situ, *1918*

Parlor in situ, *1918*

Cupola House Association—North Carolina's first preservation organization—was founded.

From 1918 until the 1960s, the association maintained the downstairs of the building as the town library and the upstairs as a local history museum. When a new town library was constructed, the association elected to reproduce the woodwork that had been sold to the Museum, recreating the lost interiors. The Museum provided architectural drawings and assistance where it could, and the downstairs was

restored. The building is now furnished as an historic house and is open to the public.

Because the original staircase had been left in the house to provide access to the second floor, in 1927 the Museum hired Frank E. Muth, an Edenton contractor, to reproduce the staircase as it then appeared. When the house in Edenton was restored in the 1960s, it was discovered that the lowest tread of the staircase originally had a curved end. Presumably the railing terminated in a spiral. These features have been

restored in the original house but not in the Museum installation.

Heavily pedimented doorways flanked by fluted pilasters lead from the stairhall to the parlor on the left and the hall on the right. In a symmetrical house, such doors would have been opposite one another. In this case, the lack of a symmetrical arrangement gives further evidence that the interior woodwork was superimposed on an earlier structure.

When the stairhall was installed in 1929, a dark brown stain was used to

Stairhall in situ *after 1960s renovation*

cover the woodwork. In 1980 paint tests revealed that the wood had at sometime been stripped. In an effort to exhibit the range of paint treatments used in the eighteenth century, two colors—brown and yellow—were applied. Use of more than one color was a popular technique both in England and the colonies, and here the two colors enrich the details of the carving and emphasize the scale of the architectural elements.

In the Museum, the Cupola House stairhall serves as a public passage through the rooms. Consequently, it is shown with no furnishings. In the eighteenth century, however, such a space would have been used for activities of daily living as well as for storage.

The fully paneled hall is the most elaborate room in the house, and as such was probably used for important functions and entertainments. The scheme of the over-mantel seems to be from a pattern shown in William Salmon's *Palladio Londonensis*, which

was also the inspiration for the fireplace in the Museum's Russell House parlor (see pp. 22-28). The pediment of the over-mantel extends into the ceiling, yet another indication that the interior woodwork was installed in an older structure.

For the 1980 renovation the bright blue which originally covered the walls of the hall was reproduced. An expensive pigment known as Prussian blue, this color was advertised in eighteenth-century newspapers and was used in the important rooms of such stylish houses as George Washington's home at Mount Vernon. The earliest layer of paint found in the hall's cupboard was also Prussian blue, but on top of that were several coats of a red-orange. The cupboard was repainted that color in order to illustrate a common eighteenth-century practice.

The hall is shown as if an afternoon rout—a party featuring sweets and wines—were in progress. The English glass pyramid, two stacked salvers with

Stairhall in The Brooklyn Museum, 1980 renovation

lly glasses, was used for serving elatin desserts at routs and other ntertainments. A similar example ppears in a contemporary English ade card illustrated here. That laborate English glassware was nported in large quantities is dicated by such historical ocumentation as a 1770 Williamsburg, irginia, inventory which includes "412 ieces of glass for pyramids, etc."

eft:
ramid—Two Stacked Salvers with lly Glasses (set of twelve). Salvers, *rca 1770; Jelly Glasses, circa 1790 ngland; glass nonymous Fund, 79.171.1-2 & .172.1-12)*

ight:
aydwell and Windle's Trade Card 70s detail) ngland; engraving ollection: Cora Ginsburg, New York

all 1980 renovation

PHOTOS: PAUL WARCHOL

Because the room is shown in use, the furniture is drawn to the center. The four tassel-back chairs with elaborately carved splats, square seats, worked or carved legs, and claw and ball feet, are typical of the Chippendale style. They date to between 1760 and 1780, and tradition has it that they belonged originally to Thomas Gibbs of Madison, New Jersey.

The marble-top mixing table between the windows, with its symmetrical curved or crooked legs terminating in pointed pad feet, is characteristic of the Queen Anne style and probably dates to between 1740 and 1770. The feet and skirt relate the table to furniture made in Rhode Island. The marble top was not only decorative and luxurious but also practical for the mixing of punches and other beverages.

The wide variety of English ceramics and glass, as well as the Chinese export porcelain shown in use throughout the room and in the cupboard, illustrates the range of wares imported by American colonists in the eighteenth century. The silver is also eighteenth-century English, as are the transfer-printed paintings on glass hanging between the windows. These paintings, portraits of King George III and Queen Charlotte, suggest that colonists prior to the Revolution considered themselves Englishmen living in America and strongly maintained their English identities.

On the floor of the hall is a painted canvas floorcloth. Although painted floorcloths are almost unknown today, they were common in eighteenth-century decoration in both America and England. Made by covering sturdy

Charles Philips
The Strong Family *1732*
Oil on canvas
Collection: The Metropolitan Museum of Art (Gift of Robert Lehman, 1944)
This portrait depicts an elaborate mantel and sconces comparable to those in the Cupola House hall and shows the English fashions that Frances Corbin, one of the Cupola House's early owners, probably tried to emulate.

Chair *1760-80*
(from a set of four originally from a larger set)
New York; mahogany
(The Dick S. Ramsay Fund, 62.3.1)

Side Table *1740-70*
Rhode Island; walnut
(25.815)

Tea Caddies *1746-47*
Made by Humphrey Payne, London;
silver
(Gift of Reverend Alfred Duane Pell,
26.811.3-5)

Dish *circa 1755*
Bow, England; soft-paste porcelain
(Gift of Mr. and Mrs. Donald S.
Morrison,
61.232.14)

W. Panther
(after oil paintings by Thomas Frye)
King George III *and* **Queen Charlotte**
circa 1760
England; transfer print on glass
(H. Randolph Lever Fund, 67.75a-b)

canvas with many layers of paint, they had hard and smooth surfaces and could be either plain or decorated like the imitation-marble reproduction used here. The work of professionals, they were first produced in England and imported to America. By the second quarter of the eighteenth century, however, most American cities had at least one maker of painted carpets, and upholsterers, paperhangers, sign painters, and house painters all advertised floorcloths in newspapers. Inventories, bills of sale, and household accounts show that they were often used in entries, passages, and halls, and on stairs, indicating that they were thought durable and were considered appropriate for areas of heavy use. Since so few have survived, it is difficult to know what patterns were the most popular. Pattern books and written descriptions, however, give a good idea of the wide range of designs and vivid colors available. The reproduction cloth shown here is based on designs by John Carwitham published in

London in 1739. Although there is no known extant cloth like it, it captures the colors and patterns which might have been available in the 1750s or '60s.

Venetian blinds hang in the windows. Blinds of this type were available in America from the 1760s and were usually painted—green was especially popular. Used to control the effects of sunlight, they protected textile and furniture surfaces. Governor Botetourt used them at the Governor's Palace in Williamsburg in 1770, and they were also used in Independence Hall in Philadelphia.

Across from the hall is the parlor. While the woodwork on this room's

Right:
Plates from Floor-Decorations of Various Kinds . . . Adapted to the Ornamenting of Halls, Rooms, Summer-houses, & etc. . . . , *designed and engraved by John Carwitham, London, 1739*
Collection: Library of Congress

Cupola House parlor 1980 renovation   PHOTO: PAUL WARCHOL

Spinet circa 1725
Made by Thomas Hitchcock, London;
walnut (base of American pine)
(The Woodward Memorial Funds,
20.897)

Card Table 1760-80
New York; mahogany
(Gift of Mrs. J. Amory Haskell,
42.118.2)

replace wall is elaborate, a chair rail
the only woodwork on the other
alls. The over-mantel here does not
netrate the ceiling as does the one in
e hall, but it still seems cramped for
e height of the room. Paint analysis
owed that the earliest colors were
hite and Prussian blue. Frequently in
e eighteenth century, white
oodwork was used with brightly
lored wallpaper. But since it was
possible to determine whether the
hite layer was a primer or an original
lor, the Prussian blue was used.
   In contrast to the hall, the room is
ranged as if not in use, with both the
airs and the tables placed around the
alls. The earliest object here is the
nglish spinet between the windows,
hich dates to the early eighteenth
ntury. Although it bears the label of
homas Hitchcock of London, the
ood of its turned frame has been
entified as American white pine.
   The tea table to the left of the
replace and the card table to the right
th date to between 1760 and 1780.
he gadrooned, undulating front and
des and the leaf-carved cabriole legs
rminating in claw and ball feet relate
e card table to a substantial group
nown to have been made in New York.
   All of the seating in the parlor is
pholstered, an indication of a wealthy

household in eighteenth-century America. Upholstered furniture was well beyond the means of the vast majority of Americans, but for those who could afford it, upholstery became an important part of decoration in the second half of the eighteenth century.

The most common fabric for covering furniture was wool. Fine wool damasks woven with baroque leaf and flower motifs were among the most expensive fabrics used for upholstery, and the reproductions shown here indicate the type of imported damasks used by Americans. Very bright colors for upholstery are often mentioned in eighteenth-century written sources, and yellow was an especially popular color. The use of the highly polished brass tacks and the cushions are suggested by John Singleton Copley's *Portrait of an Unknown Woman*, painted in 1771.

The window curtains, which are made of the same wool damask, are similar to what are now known as Austrian shades. This design, published as early as 1700, was used extensively in both England and America and is often seen in contemporary paintings and prints. Curtains were uncommon in the eighteenth century and were usually found only in the houses of the wealthy. Where they were used, it was customary to have them match the upholstery.

The needlework carpet on the floor is English and dates to between 1750 and 1775. An example of ladies' needlework, it features an especially fine bold floral design and is in excellent condition. It is known from Corbin's estate sale that he owned a Wilton carpet. Although there is no documentation for English needlework carpets in America, this carpet has been used as a replacement.

Off the central stairhall and behind the parlor is a room furnished as a downstairs chamber. Its woodwork, which consists of a fireplace mantel and a chair rail, is more delicate and

John Singleton Copley
Portrait of an Unknown Woman,
1771 Oil on canvas

Cupola House parlor *1980 renovation*   PHOTO: PAUL WARCHOL

restrained than that of the front two rooms, and points to a later date, perhaps 1790 to 1810.

In the corner to the right of the chamber's fireplace is a Massachusetts Queen Anne easy chair dating to between 1740 and 1760. This chair is especially remarkable for the survival of its original upholstery, a red wool moreen. For purposes of preservation, in the 1980 renovation a slipcover was fabricated to preserve the original fabric. Slipcovers were commonly utilized in the eighteenth century to protect more expensive upholstery.

In the corner to the left of the fireplace is a Rhode Island armchair

Right:
Easy Chair *1740-60*
Massachusetts; walnut
(Henry L. Batterman, Carll H. DeSilver, Maria L. Emmons, and Charles S. Smith Funds, 32.38)
This chair is shown with its original upholstery.

pola House chamber *1980 renovation*   PHOTOS: PAUL WARCHOL

upola House chamber 1980 *renovation*   PHOTO: PAUL WARCHOL

Artist Unknown (English)
Lady Friz at her Toilet
circa 1777-79
Engraving
Collection: Yale University
(Print Collection, Lewis Walpole
Library)

which for many years was shown as a desk chair in another of the Museum's period rooms. In 1980 it was restored to its original function as a commode. The pewter chamber pot that it holds was made by Frederick Bassett, who worked in New York City and Hartford, Connecticut, between 1761 and 1800.

Between the windows opposite the bed is a dressing table that dates to between 1750 and 1800 and was probably made in New England. In colonial America, where there were few dressing rooms, chambers were often fitted with dressing tables, sometimes *en suite* with other case pieces. Middle-class Americans often used tables like the one shown in the 1770s English fashion print illustrated here.

During the seventeenth and eighteenth centuries large quantities of printed cotton and linen were imported to America from England. These fabrics were used in bed-hangings,

acing page:
antry 1980 renovation
HOTO: PAUL WARCHOL

below:
C. Collier (d. 1702 or before)
Trompe l'Oeil with Writing Materials
Oil on canvas
Collection: Victoria and Albert Museum,
London

clothing, slipcovers, and counterpanes. By 1750 printed cottons began to reflect the growing influence of the Rococo, and designs became lighter with flowers and naturalistic forms arranged in asymmetrical patterns. The modern fabric used here reproduces the popular eighteenth-century florals that embodied a new taste for the less formal.

Across the stairhall from the chamber is a small pantry/office. Although it was erected with the rest of the rooms in 1929, there is no record of it having been opened or furnished. From the pantry two doors lead into the main entertainment room, the hall. There was also easy access to the stairhall and out the back door to a detached kitchen at the rear of the house. The pantry was thus a staging area for serving. Kitchens were often detached in larger houses in order to prevent fire in the main house and to keep cooking odors from offending family and guests.

Although no evidence survives for the eighteenth-century arrangement of the room, simple shelves have been constructed to suggest a storage area for more valuable foodstuffs and frequently used eating implements. The room's second function as an office is indicated by the desk between the windows. Above the desk is a letter-holder made of woven tape. Precursors of the modern bulletin board, such letter-holders appeared in genre paintings from at least 1700.

The Cupola House has been furnished in an attempt to convey the taste and life-style of an affluent colonist in a small Southern port. Furniture imported from the Northern colonies, as well as other goods from abroad, suggests the desire to display newly found wealth.

Cane Acres Plantation Dining Room 1980 renovation   PHOTO: PAUL WARCHOL

THE SOUTH

Cane Acres Plantation
CIRCA *1799–1806*

Summerville, South Carolina

As installed in the Brooklyn Museum, the dining room from the Cane Acres Plantation House exemplifies the concept of a unified taste that evolved in Federal America from the time of the Revolution through the nineteenth century. During the early eighteenth century, when each room was used for a variety of functions, the range of objects furnishing a room was an eclectic mix, based not so much on taste or style as on necessity. The introduction of rooms used specifically for dining in the Federal period led to the development of new furniture forms such as sideboards and large dining tables. This coincided with the popularity of an attenuated Classical style of decoration on furniture and woodwork so that a room and its contents presented a unified statement.

Cane Acres Plantation was located in the low country twenty-four miles northwest of Charleston, the major cultural, social, and commercial center of South Carolina. Records reveal that Edward Tongue purchased Cane Acres in 1789 and that by 1799 a house was standing on the property. The woodwork now in the Museum may be from that or a slightly later house; the date or numbers 1806 was found in three different locations when it was removed from the house.

Cane Acres was one of many plantations in the area producing rich yields of rice and sugar. In most cases the houses on these plantations were not year-round residences because of the unbearable heat and the fear of the swamps, thought to be the cause of malaria. During the most uncomfortable months planters visited spas in the North or sought the cooler sea breezes in Charleston, where many of them maintained homes.

Above:
This photograph of a watercolor of Cane Acres Plantation (artist and date unknown) was given to the Museum in 1931 by Mrs. Heyward Haskell, a granddaughter of James Perry, one of the plantation's owners.

Below:
This exterior photograph of the plantation house was taken by D. Y. Lenhart in 1946 for The West Virginia Pulp and Paper Company. A short time later the shell of the house either collapsed or was destroyed.

The fertility of the land provided planters with the means to build large and stylish plantation houses embellished with fashionable decorations. The architecture of the house at Cane Acres reflected its tropical location. The large two-story frame structure rested on a brick foundation, high enough to avoid flooding and to catch the breeze. Windows were plentiful and arranged to provide the best ventilation possible.

While the interior of the house reflected the latest in regional Classical woodwork, the exterior was a late-Georgian rectangular block. The central entry was flanked by sidelights and topped by a fan window, a delicate reinterpretation of eighteenth-century elements characteristic of the Federal period. The term Federal refers to the roughly three decades following the American Revolution, the period of the new Federal Government. The Federal style was the American response to Neoclassicism as advocated by the English designer Robert Adam.

Cane Acres Plantation descended in the family of Edward Tongue until 1852, when a prominent Charlestonian named James Perry purchased the property. The Perry family owned the plantation until 1904, and between 1904 and 1924 the land and the house were owned by a series of lumber companies. Allowed to deteriorate, the house was occupied by squatters who apparently utilized much of the interior finish for firewood. In 1924, the owner, The West Virginia Pulp and Paper Company, invited the Museum to salvage the woodwork.

Andre Rueff, the Assistant Curator of Decorative Arts, was dispatched to supervise its removal. The house was in a state of near ruin. Rather than removing a single room, Rueff took most of two rooms and whatever else was intact or nearly so. (In addition to the dining room, the entrance vestibule to the Cane Acres installation has woodwork from the house.)

Because the house was in such an advanced state of decay, it was difficult for Rueff to mark pieces for use in reconstruction. A film development error rendered poor if not useless photographs. In fact, the entire operation was frought with difficulties Rueff had not encountered or at least reported in previous dismantlings.

Situated in the middle of a forest planted by The West Virginia Pulp and Paper Company, the house was virtually inaccessible. In a report written after his return to Brooklyn, Rueff described the conditions:

"The road to it is a soft, sandy highway for about seven miles, after which there is a 'country road'

Top right:
Dining Room from White Hall
a house built by Thomas Porcher in the Santee-Cooper River Valley of South Carolina about 1818
Collection: The Museum of Early Southern Decorative Arts, Winston-Salem, North Carolina

(it is so called by the natives) but it is really but a way cut through a swamp by lumbermen several years ago, corduroyed on what then were the worst places, awash most of the way and a foot and a half under water occasionally. The travelling on these last eight miles was always bad: we covered it in a Ford car—Fords and mules are the only modes of locomotion in such country—at low speed all the time."

Rueff wrote that because of "the statement of my carpenter that 'the road is good yet, but wait till the rain comes, and you won't take anything,' I lost not (sic) time in measuring, photographing all I had to remove."

The prophecy of the carpenter proved nearly correct. The night before the first departure with the material the rains came, and Rueff had troubles on the "country road:"

"A former rice field washed away some fifty feet of it, but a nearby log house in fairly good condition provided the necessary lumber for bridging the spot—until a later rain floated the logs, which rolled away while a truck of bricks was passing . . . the first truckload—only 400 bricks—bogged, stuck, had to be partially unloaded and finally arrived at the freight station with about 250 left. The lumber trucks, used for cornices, wainscoting and flooring fared not better: they had to be unloaded, the pieces carried by hand, and reloaded after passing over the bad section. The mule teams had no greater success: either the poles broke or something else did."

It could not have been surprising that after the experience "some of the truckmen refused to return." However, others did, and in three days all salvageable material had been removed from the site.

The spacious room now in The Brooklyn Museum was off the central stairhall and extended from the front to the back of the house. The center windows at either end were eliminated in the 1929 installation probably to provide wall space for furniture. The generous proportions of the room and the number of windows reflect the semi-tropical location of the house and the fact that heating was not a problem.

Above: ***Cane Acres Dining Room*** *1940s installation*   Below: *1960s installation*

Cane Acres Plantation Dining Room *1980 renovation*　　　PHOTO: PAUL WARCHOL

Though the room is much larger than the Museum's eighteenth-century period rooms, the scale of the carved decoration on its woodwork is much smaller. The shallow chip-carved decorations in the cornices are fanned ovals and swags—basic design vocabulary of the period simplified to the training and background of a local craftsman.

Similar woodwork, possibly carved by the same hand, is now installed in a period dining room in the Museum of Early Southern Decorative Arts in Winston-Salem, North Carolina. It was taken from a house called White Hall that was built by Thomas Porcher in the Santee-Cooper River Valley of South Carolina about 1818.

The Cane Acres Dining Room demonstrates not only an emerging taste, but also a change in the life-style of affluent Americans. Although great dining halls and rooms were not unusual in the palaces and great houses of Europe, a separate dining room was a new notion in Federal America. This was the beginning of specific room usage, and over the next two centuries, rooms and furniture forms became associated with particular functions. As more and more Americans in the twentieth century turn to apartment living, this evolution may reverse itself in the next century.

English designers and decorators like Thomas Sheraton and George Hepplewhite published books of furniture designs, and cabinetmakers in Federal America eagerly utilized these books to create furniture for the country's new dining rooms. Perhaps the most significant form introduced in the period was the sideboard, a case piece which was used for the storage of wine and utensils as well as for serving. Large extension or sectional tables replaced the smaller tilt-top tables of the eighteenth century. Since Federal furniture was widely sought after among collectors in the 1920s, the Cane Acres Dining Room was one of the Museum's most admired interiors when the series opened in 1929.

Although few changes have been made in the furniture of the room, the room's aura has changed as twentieth-century taste and scholarship have evolved. Tests for original paint colors have been inconclusive, but in the 1940s John Graham selected the lavender and buff gray, colors popular in the first quarter of the nineteenth century. In the early 1960s, when a new ceiling was required, the installation was reevaluated. A huge gilt chandelier replaced a small fixture in the center of the ceiling; a French Aubusson carpet was laid on the floor beneath the table; and sheer swags, Classical in form, replaced heavy damask drapes at the windows. The overall effect was urbane, elegant, and very French. In her much publicized renovation of The White House at the time, First Lady Jacqueline Kennedy was popularizing this look with her work on that building dating to the same period as Cane Acres.

In the 1980 renovation, one of the major changes in the room was its name. Since its acquisition by the Museum in 1924, the room had been called the Perry Plantation Dining Room. But research undertaken by Columbia University graduate students determined that the prominent Perry family had not owned the property until 1852. These students discovered that during the period interpreted at the Museum the place was known as Cane Acres Plantation, and that name is currently used for the installation.

In the most recent reevaluation of the room, the location of the plantation in the low country, and its status as a part-time residence, were considered, and the room was considerably simplified. The dominating chandelier was removed not only because it was considered inappropriate for an American house of the period, much less a country one, but also because it destroyed the airiness and spaciousness of the large interior.

Considered equally inappropriate for a country place, the Aubusson carpet was replaced with a green canvas floorcloth. Floorcloths, important in eighteenth-century decoration, continued to be popular well into the nineteenth century. Plain floorcloths seem to have been used in great numbers, and written sources reveal they could be of almost any dimension from quite small to room size. The green floorcloth shown here would have protected the floor around the table from wear and dirt. An inventory of The White House taken in 1809 during Thomas Jefferson's Presidency notes several canvas floorcloths painted green, including one in "the small dining room."

Window treatments were abandoned in favor of suggesting the climate of the region and to establish that curtains and draperies were not common in the United States until the mid-nineteenth century. The bookcase at the end of the dining room, utilized as a china cupboard in former installations, was returned to its original function. Bookcases with glazed doors were commonly draped to protect the bindings of the volumes.

The furniture in the room is all of the Federal period, *circa* 1790–1810. The style is characterized by broad smooth surfaces of highly figured veneers on case pieces and tables. These veneers

Card Table 1790–1810
Baltimore; mahogany with inlaid decoration
(H. Randolph Lever Fund, 73.14.3)

Above:
Detail of card table top

Tall Clock circa *1800*
Made by Effingham Embree, New York;
mahogany with inlaid decoration
and brass finials
(Gift of Mrs. Teunis Schenck, 63.97)

Chair circa *1800*
New York; mahogany
(H. Randolph Lever Fund, 77.48.3)

were decorated with inlay and stringing of exotic woods in tight compositions of ovals, circles, and squares. The semi-circular card table made in Baltimore between 1790 and 1810 is an outstanding example of this style. It has a top beautifully inlaid in spokes radiating from a central inlaid leaf design at the back center—a pattern similar to the fan windows which crowned main entrances to Federal houses. The table's legs are square, tapered from top to bottom, and decorated with bellflower inlay—a popular motif of the period.

Coastal trade was extensive between Charleston and the urban North during the period, and advertisements in Charleston newspapers document ships coming from New York with quantities of furniture probably made in that city. Consequently, a number of New York objects have been included in the installation. The mahogany side chair, with its shield back derived from English design books, is a familiar form made in both New York and Charleston, and the tall clock bears the label of Effingham Embree of New York City on its face. The clock's case is decorated above the dial with an inlaid American eagle, one of the patriotic symbols that became a part of the decorative vocabulary of craftsmen working in Federal America. Reeded quarter columns on the front corners of the case and the Classical arch of the hood supported by reeded columns lend the clock an architectural sense.

The large gilt mirror hanging in the center of the side wall is probably also from New York. It is decorated at its top with an *eglomisé* panel. This reverse painting on glass, though an old technique, was introduced as decoration for furniture during the Federal period. The crowning eagle supporting swags of gilt chains and beads was a popular finial for these mirrors.

Despite the Revolution, affluent Americans resumed buying luxury goods from England once hostilities ceased. The pair of silver plated Argand lamps on the sideboard are typical of these expensive imports. They represent an innovation in lighting, for their improved ventilation made fuel burn longer and brighter. The Classical center urns which held the fuel relate to the overall Neoclassical feeling of the room.

Throughout the colonial period, Chinese export porcelains had come to America through London agents. But with independence a direct trade between China and the new United States developed and flourished. While the noble families of Europe had long commissioned porcelain dinner services incorporating coats of arms as a central decoration, in democratic America standard motifs were used. The blue-and-gilt draped shield on the Cane Acres room's service incorporates the initials of the Jackson family of Brooklyn. Services in this pattern were ordered by affluent families all along the Eastern seaboard during the Federal period. Here, the service is set on the table for the dessert and fruit course of a dinner. For this course, the white linen tablecloth was generally removed—a practice which can be seen in the painting *The Dinner Party* by Henry Sargent.

Facing page, top:
Fruit Basket and Stand circa *1780*
(part of a 215-piece service)
China; porcelain
(Gift of Mrs. William Sterling Peters, 48.207.189 & 48.207.191)

Facing page, bottom:
Henry Sargent
The Dinner Party circa *1821*
Oil on canvas
Collection: Museum of Fine Arts, Boston (Gift of Mrs. Horatio A. Lamb in memory of Mr. and Mrs. Winthrop Sargent)

Above:
Mirror *1790–1810*
New York; wood with gesso and gilt
(H. Randolph Lever Fund, 71.149.3)

Right:
Argand Lamps circa *1800*
England; silver plate
(59.82.a–b)

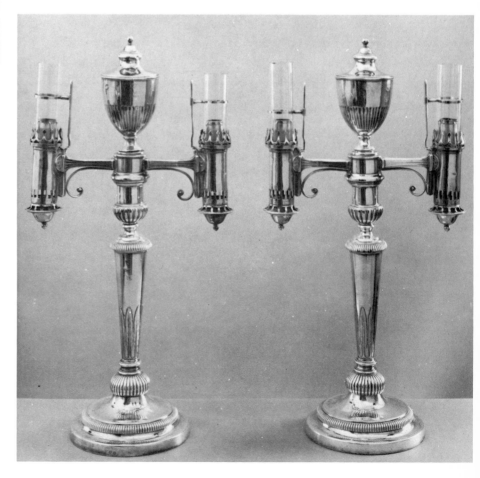

Entries shown in bold italics refer to The Brooklyn Museum.

*indicates works in the collection of The Brooklyn Museum not yet installed in 1983.

Circa **1850** Ben: Perley Poore (1820-1887) displays his private collection of ceramics, pewter, metalware, furniture, and architectural elements in period room settings at his home Indian Hill in West Newbury, Massachusetts.

1864 A New England kitchen displayed at a fair held in Brooklyn by The Sanitary Commission (a foreruner of the Red Cross) attracts popular attention.

1873 Artur Hazelius founds the Nordiska Museet in Stockholm, Sweden, displaying arts and crafts in vignettes or tableux similar to those found in wax museums.

1876 The Centennial Exposition in Philadelphia includes a Connecticut Cottage and an Old Log Cabin New England Kitchen among its many exhibits. Their popularity marks a turning point in the public's awareness of America's Colonial past.

1880 Period settings of a kitchen, a parlor, and a chamber are included in displays at the Memorial Hall Museum in Deerfield, Massachusetts (a history museum housed in a 1798 building of the Deerfield Academy).

1891 Skansen—the first outdoor museum—opens in a seventy-five acre park in Stockholm. Established by Artur Hazelius, the museum includes complete historic houses brought to the site, and costumed guides demonstrating various crafts and daily routines.

1906 The Museum of Art, Rhode Island School of Design, in Providence opens the Charles L. Pendleton Collection of American Decorative Arts in a Georgian house specifically designed to accommodate it.

The first major exhibit of American decorative arts, *American Silver: The Work of Seventeenth and Eighteenth Century Silversmiths,* is held at the Museum of Fine Arts in Boston.

1907 Three period room alcoves are installed at the Essex Institute in Salem, Massachusetts. A local history museum, the Institute today includes six historic houses ranging in date from 1684 to 1818.

1908 Henry Davis Sleeper, a Boston interior designer, begins to install woodwork from old houses of various periods in his home Beauport at Gloucester Harbor, Massachusetts (the home is now owned by the Society for the Preservation of New England Antiquities).

1909 The first major comprehensive exhibition of American decorative arts, a survey of the years 1625 to 1825 entitled *The Hudson-Fulton Exhibition*, is held at the Metropolitan Museum of Art in New York. The public success of this experimental exhibition, and the Metropolitan's purchase of the H. Eugene Bolles Collection from it, gives legitimacy to the collecting of American decorative arts by museums.

1910 The Metropolitan Museum of Art acquires its first woodwork (from the Hewlett House in Woodbury, Long Island).

1914 *Luke Vincent Lockwood—pioneer scholar and collector of Americana—is elected to the Board of Governors of The Brooklyn Museum. A Department of Colonial and Early-American Furniture is established during his first year.*

1915 *The Brooklyn Museum acquires its first paneling (from a dealer in Danbury, Connecticut).*

1917 *The Museum acquires the entire groundfloor woodwork from the Henry Trippe House in Secretary, Maryland, and the woodwork from two front parlors of the Porter-Belden House in Wethersfield, Connecticut.*

1918 *The groundfloor woodwork of the Cupola House in Edenton, North Carolina, is acquired by the Museum.*

1920 *The woodwork from the front parlor of the Russell House in Providence, Rhode Island, is acquired by the Museum.*

1922 *The Museum acquires the woodwork from the upstairs chamber of the Bliss House in Springfield, Massachusetts.*

1924 The Metropolitan Museum of Art opens its new American Wing, becoming the first American art museum to organize a large and systematic collection of period rooms.

Woodwork from the dining room of the Cane Acres Plantation in Summerville, South Carolina, and from the parlor, stairhall*, and dining room of a house (circa 1820) in Irvington, New Jersey, is acquired by the Museum.

1926 Colonial Williamsburg, Virginia, is founded, and restoration work begins there with funds donated by John D. Rockefeller. Today, this on-site preservation of the former Virginia capital comprises fifty-eight restored buildings dating from 1693 to 1837, and fifty reconstructed eighteenth-century buildings.

1928 The Museum of Fine Arts in Boston opens a decorative arts wing including period rooms.

The Philadelphia Museum of Art opens a group of American period rooms.

1929 *The Brooklyn Museum acquires the entire groundfloor woodwork of the local Nicholas Schenck House (circa 1770) and opens nineteen American period rooms ranging in date from the 1720s to the 1820s.*

The Greenfield Village and Henry Ford Museum is founded at Dearborn, Michigan. This village museum of American history today includes a hundred historic structures dating from the seventeenth to the twentieth century.

1930 American period rooms are opened at the Baltimore Museum of Art and the St. Louis Art Museum (1930-31).

1940 *The Brooklyn Museum acquires the hall* and front parlor* woodwork of the local Matthew Clarkson, Jr., House (circa 1836) and the woodwork from two parlors of the 1853 Robert J. Milligan House in Saratoga Springs, New York.*

1941 *The Museum acquires the woodwork from the library* of New York City's Sloane-Griswold House, designed by the Herter Brothers in 1882.*

1946 *The woodwork from the Moorish smoking room (circa 1877) of New York City's John D. Rockefeller House is acquired by the Museum.*

Old Sturbridge Village, Massachusetts, opens to the public. An outdoor living-history museum, the Village today consists of more than forty historical buildings.

1947 Plymouth Plantation, Massachusetts—an outdoor living-history museum and Pilgrim village—opens to the public.

The Shelburne Museum in Vermont opens. Today, this general museum is housed in thirty-five early-American buildings situated on a hundred-acre site.

1951 Delaware's Henry Francis du Pont Winterthur Museum (incorporated in 1930) opens to the public. It includes an extensive collection of American decorative arts installed in period rooms.

1952 *The Brooklyn Museum acquires the entire Jan Martense Schenck House (circa 1675) in Flatlands, Brooklyn.*

Historic Deerfield, Massachusetts, is founded by Mr. and Mrs. Henry Flynt. This history museum today consists of twelve buildings of eighteenth- and early nineteenth-century origin.

1953 *The Brooklyn Museum is the first American art museum to open a series of nineteenth-century period rooms: the parlor and library from the Robert J. Milligan House; a Civil War dressing room alcove; and the Moorish smoking room from the John D. Rockefeller House.*

1964 *The Museum installs the complete ground floor of the Jan Martense Schenck House—the earliest house in its series.*

1966 The Bayou Bend Collection in Houston, Texas, opens. Given to Houston's Museum of Fine Arts in 1958 by Ima Hogg, it is the first (and only) museum of American decorative arts in the Southwest.

1971 *The Brooklyn Museum opens the Worgelt Library (1928-30), an Art Deco room from New York City.*

1973 The new installation of the Mabel Brady Garvan Galleries of the Yale University Art Gallery in New Haven, Connecticut, rejects the period room approach in favor of an installation that focuses attention on the individual object while inviting comparisons of style, structure, and regional characteristics.

1980 *The Brooklyn Museum acquires the entrance hall woodwork* of New York City's Edward Dean Adams House (circa 1886), one of the Villard Houses complex designed by McKim, Mead and White.*

Right:
Chamber
The Porter-Belden House
Wethersfield, Connecticut
Circa *1760-1800*

Back cover:
Parlor
The Porter-Belden House
Wethersfield, Connecticut
Circa *1760-1800*

The Brooklyn Museum Period Rooms Acquisition Credits

NEW ENGLAND

The Danbury Alcove
Connecticut
18th Century
Henry L. Batterman Fund
15.511

The Reuben Bliss House
Springfield, Massachusetts
Circa 1750
Alfred T. White Memorial Fund and Samuel E. Haslett Estate Funds
22.1936

The Porter-Belden House
Wethersfield, Connecticut
Circa 1760–1800
Charles Stewart Smith Memorial Fund
17.129

The Russell House
Providence, Rhode Island
Circa 1772
Gift of The Rembrandt Club
20.956

THE SOUTH

The Henry Trippe House
Secretary, Maryland
Circa 1724–31
Charles Stewart Memorial Fund
17.130

The Cupola House
Edenton, North Carolina
Circa 1725
(Woodwork 1756–58)
Robert B. Woodward Memorial Fund
18.170

Cane Acres Plantation
Summerville, South Carolina
Circa 1799–1806
Gift of The West Virginia Pulp and Paper Company
24.421

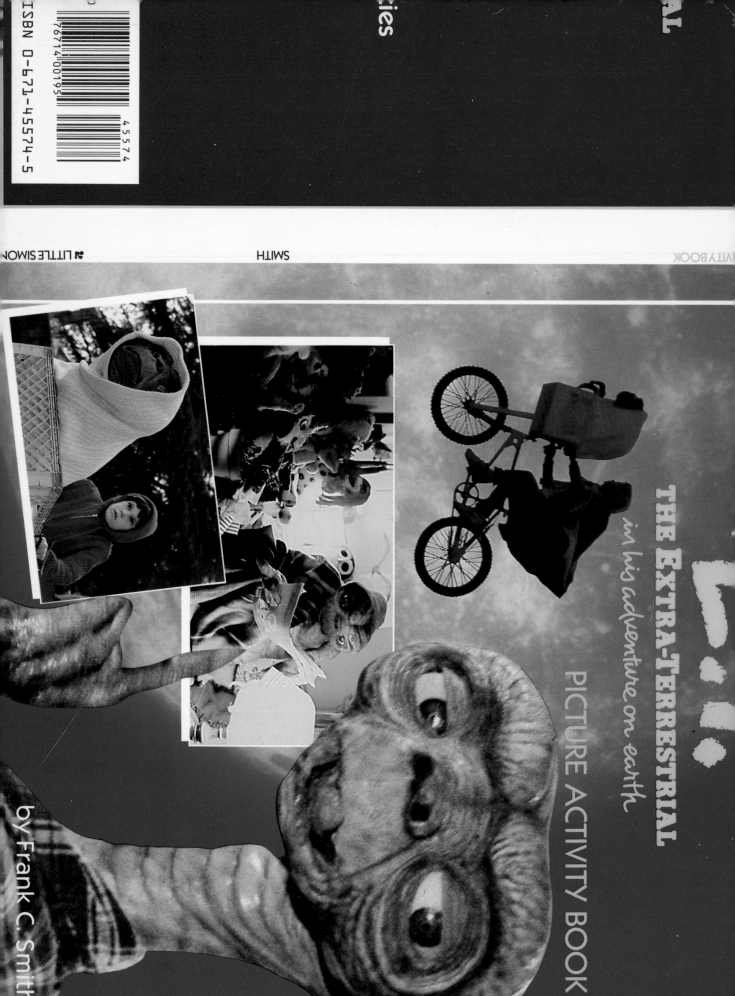